A CENTURY AROUND SILLOTH

By Peter Ostle and Stephen Wright

with Josephine Best, John Molyneux, Helen Nattrass, Terry Nave and Karen Simpson of the Holme St Cuthbert History Group

P3 Publications

Website: www.p3publications.com   Email: dave@p3publications.com

This book is dedicated with many, many happy memories to

Winnie Bell   *Betty Connolly*   *Eric Laws*
(1918 – 2011)   *(1932 – 2011)*   *(1912 – 2010)*

ISBN 978-0-9572412-3-7

Copyright © 2012 Stephen Wright & Peter Ostle

First published in the UK by:

P3 Publications
13 Beaver Road
Carlisle
Cumbria
CA2 7PS

Printed in the UK at:

The Amadeus Press
Ezra House
West 26 Business Park
Cleckheaton
BD19 4TQ

CONTENTS

Page

Sketches by Josephine Best - - - Aerial photography (page 45) by Simon Ledingham
Front Cover: Bessie Lomas, Silloth's fishmonger for many years.
Back Cover: Lofty Stoddart, Hell Driver.
Solway Sunset by David Ramshaw

HOLME ST CUTHBERT HISTORY GROUP
Email: plain.people@yahoo.co.uk
Website: www.solwayplain.co.uk

A Tribute

Before presenting the book, we really have to acknowledge two people who played a big role in documenting life on the Solway Plain over the twentieth century.

The first is Mr Sydney Martin. Sydney took hundreds of photographs during his career, running one of Silloth's most prominent shops which he took over from his father, John Martin, who passed away suddenly in 1907.

Sydney and wife, Hilda, ran Martins newsagents for a good part of the century. Wearing several different hats – printer, stationer, fancy goods dealer and photographer – Sydney contributed much to the business life of Silloth. His main legacy is the photographic postcards which he made, illustrating life in Silloth and other local places for over fifty years. Although not the only local photographer, he seems to have taken the largest number of views, some of which are expensive collectors' items today.

Sydney developed the images in a special room above the shop, before sending the best ones away to printers such as Sankey of Barrow and Valentine of Dundee. They made postcards from them and sent batches of them back to be sold in the shop. Since then they have found their way all over the world.

Hilda and Sydney Martin

The second person we must thank is Bessie Winter. She and her husband, Jack, had worked in the Martins' shop since 1953 and, after 10 years, they became the proprietors. Although the photography ceased and, indeed, sales and production of postcards fell steadily from the 60s onward, in her later years, Bessie became very interested in Silloth's history.

Using the large Martin archive as a start, she built up a collection of photos, news articles and ephemera spanning Silloth's history, some of which were displayed for everyone in the shop windows.
Bessie passed away, after a long illness, in 2003, leaving an extensive local history collection. Our thanks are due to her family for making this material available to us.

About the book

This is a companion volume to the two previous Plain People books. These concentrated on the rural area of the plain. This one focuses on the town of Silloth, the main centre of population, and covers only the twentieth century.
It is by no means a full account of the century; we have selected the most important and significant events and tried to tell the story of these years through the lives of the people involved.
There were many things about which we were unable to find adequate information, illustrations or memories. We are really sorry we couldn't include them all.

CHAPTER ONE

1900 – 1914, The Edwardian Era

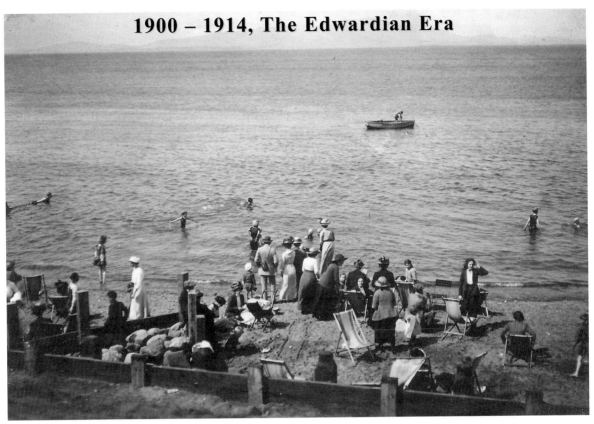

Some rather formally dressed visitors on the shore at Silloth.

In photographs from the Edwardian era, it seems the sun is always shining. The women are all elegantly dressed. The men look prosperous and self-confident. This is England in the Age of Empire.

Indeed, it was a very comfortable time for those with money and it is they who feature in the photographs. British society was still completely divided along class lines. There are few pictures of working men or their families. Photography was a luxury they couldn't afford.

In his book *'The Edwardians'*, Roy Hattersley quotes several surveys taken around this time. These set a poverty line – the weekly income needed to support a family on a healthy diet – at £1.08 for urban workers. It was lower, at 95p, for their rural counterparts who could grow their own vegetables and keep a few hens.

In 1901, Wigton Rural District Council reported on farm labourers' wages in the area. Single men were receiving 62p a week. A married man could expect around 90p and casual labourers got between 15p and 20p a day. Poverty was not limited to the slum areas in large cities. Most local people had a pretty tough life in these years. For the first time ever, the farmers were suffering from foreign competition. Every cargo of North American wheat landed at Silloth docks meant less work for them and their farmhands. Refrigerated ships were bringing in meat from Australia and South America.

Many families who had worked on the land for generations were leaving the rural areas and heading for better paid work in the towns. In our area, many found jobs in the coal mines. In Aspatria, an underground worker could earn almost £2.00 a week and even surface workers could expect well over a pound. Between 1901 and 1911, Aspatria's population increased by sixteen per cent. Many of these people must have moved from the area's farming communities.

As you look at our pictures of happy trippers in Silloth or the prosperous local business people, please remember these invisible men and their families. For them, things would change – but only very slowly.

Edwardian Silloth

Silloth in the early 1900s.

In 1900, Silloth was still a very new town. Fifty years previously, there had been only four farms in the area and the site of the main streets was covered in sand dunes. The railway from Carlisle arrived in 1856. The docks opened three years later.

The town, laid out on a regular grid pattern, was planned as a health resort for the upper and middle classes. Fresh air, long walks and sea bathing were the town's main attractions. For visitors "who did not care for the cold and exposure of open-air bathing" the local guide recommended a visit to the baths. Here, 100,000 gallons of fresh sea water were pumped up, by steam power, at every tide. Bathing in sea water became popular in the nineteenth century as a cure for almost everything. Martin's guide book for the period also claimed

that "the amount of ozone found in the atmosphere is much greater than at any other place in the British Isles. Ozone is oxygen in a condensed form. . . it is entirely antagonistic to all forms of impurity. Sunshine is so prevalent that the mean average temperature is, in fact, higher than many places in the south of England. This, combined with the almost complete absence of fog, renders Silloth a particularly desirable place for invalids."

Some industry had also come to the town. The Carr family, who owned a large biscuit factory in Carlisle, opened a flour mill on the side of the dock in 1886. Two chemical works, mostly producing agricultural fertilizer, were located near the railway. These businesses imported all their raw materials through the port. Their story is told in Chapter Five.

There were several large hotels in Silloth but many visitors would stay in one of the numerous boarding houses around the town. The local directory for 1901 lists 118 of these. Many familiar Silloth names occur in the list. Mrs Over had two double and one single room to let at 3, Eden Street. Mrs Lomas let three rooms at 3, Solway Street and Mrs Selkirk had four singles and a sitting room available at No. 13.

In Esk Street, Mrs Akitt offered one double, three singles and two sitting rooms.

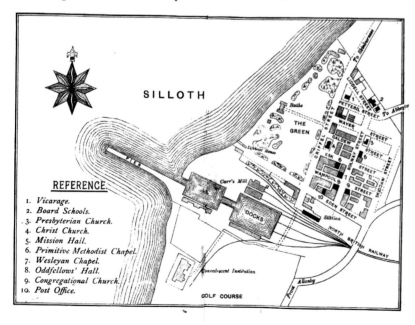

REFERENCE.
1. *Vicarage.*
2. *Board Schools.*
3. *Presbyterian Church.*
4. *Christ Church.*
5. *Mission Hall.*
6. *Primitive Methodist Chapel.*
7. *Wesleyan Chapel.*
8. *Oddfellows' Hall.*
9. *Congregational Church.*
10. *Post Office.*

A Map of the town in 1900 taken from Martin's Guide Book.

Sail and Steam

Ship Nereide at Silloth.

German full-rigger 'Nereide' brought wheat from North America via Cape Horn in 1907.

By the early twentieth century, Silloth was also well established as a port. The first decade of the twentieth century was one of its busiest; ships came from all over the world with a variety of cargoes and took away locally produced goods.

Coal was the main export, this came from mines near Aspatria and east of Carlisle; most went to the Irish market. There was a daily general cargo service to Liverpool and the SS 'Yarrow' operated a twice-weekly one to Dublin via the Isle of Man. Passengers could use both these routes.

The period saw a great change – the transition from vessels powered by the wind to those powered by steam engines. Steam powered vessels were replacing sailing ships because they could keep going regardless of wind speed or direction. Voyage times were more reliable and predictable. However, they were more costly to run and had to be kept busy in order to cover fuel costs. Cargo runs had to be maximised and time in port kept to a minimum. Although steam vessels had been developed in the early nineteenth century, it took a long time for engines to be developed which were economical over any distance. Thus sail, at least in ocean trades, held its own for a while.

By the twentieth century, steam engines were much more fuel efficient and, with a worldwide network of coaling stations established, they were becoming the preferred choice for transport.

There were still many sailing vessels around during the first two decades of the twentieth century. At Silloth, cargoes of slate were brought in by Welsh schooners. Coal was taken across the Solway to Annan and Dumfries on small sailing boats.

In the ocean trades, large barques and full rigged ships came in from Australia and America's West Coast with grain and from Canada with wood. Over very long distances, with favourable winds, sail could often outperform steam. The last foreign cargoes brought by sail were landed in 1915. Coastal sail continued in the Solway for a few more years.

The period also saw another change - the decline in the number of ocean going ships visiting Silloth. The size of ships employed in foreign trade was increasing. It was cheaper to move cargo in large amounts, and these cargo sizes were often beyond the needs of local firms. Some large ships delivered

Below right: *The SS 'Trial' in port around 1905. On the right is the coal loader.*

Below: *Small schooners such as the 'Scotia', seen here being towed out, still plied the Solway in the 1900s. Most loaded coal for harbours on the Scottish side of the Solway. This was one of the last trades to use sail.*

Steam dominates in this view taken in June 1906. The large vessel on the left, the 'Brenner', had brought wheat from Sulina, Romania. Carrs used a lot of East European wheat at this time.

part cargoes to Silloth, but mainly it was necessary to bring goods on coasters from the larger British ports where the large ships discharged foreign loads. This process is known as transhipment and an increasing amount of cargo came to Silloth this way.

One issue which affected trade at Silloth, and indeed internationally at this time, was the conflict in Turkey and Eastern Europe. Hungary and Romania were two of the world's largest wheat producers, and supplied a large portion of Britain's grain. This was loaded onto ships at ports on the Danube and Black Sea and brought to Britain via Gibraltar. Conflict in the region flared up in 1910 and put an end to this traffic.

The docks created plenty of work for the local people. More people worked there in the 1900s than at any other time. In 1901, there were 62 men employed at the docks, plus seven others in related maritime roles such as coast officer. Some worked in the 'Hydraulics', the small power station that supplied water pressure for the port equipment. Some oversaw the dock gates. The rest were mainly involved in getting cargoes in or out of the ships.

Most families in Silloth had someone who worked at the port at one time or another. However, work was not consistent. It all depended on when the ships came in – some days there was little to do. There certainly wasn't enough to keep 60 men occupied full time.

Pay was not much, and few earned a living on dock work alone. Some dockers' wives made income by letting rooms to visitors in the holiday season. Other men worked part time as fishermen or at the chemical works. A few were keen to spend what they did earn in local bars.

Timber was another foreign import, several cargoes coming from Eastern Europe during the Edwardian era.

Here we see the large steamer 'Gisella Groedel' which brought her cargo from Romania in June 1905.

In 1907, the 'Ailsa' missed the high tide and ran aground, blocking the port entrance. In the picture, a coaster is lying at anchor, unable to enter the dock and, behind the pier, the 'Yarrow' has also found her passage blocked. The tug 'Petrel' is being used to ferry the passengers ashore.

Captain Chisholm's model fleet

CAPTAIN CHISHOLMS MODEL FLEET

Above: Capt. Chisholm and family.

One man who experienced the transition from sail to steam at first hand was **Captain Duncan Chisholm**. He was the man who made beautiful models of the sailing ships which he remembered from his youth. Sidney Martin produced a special postcard of them.

Duncan was born at Carlisle in 1857. He went to sea at the age of fourteen, serving aboard the 'Silloth', the 'Albatross' and, finally, the 'Kittiwake'.

He became Chief Officer of the 'Kittiwake' and, in October 1900, helped save the crew of the barque 'Topdale' which was in difficulties on the Solway. The Liverpool Shipwreck Humane Society awarded him an illuminated address and silver medal for his part in this rescue.

Around 1903, he became captain of the Silloth paddle tug 'Petrel'. In this position, he was responsible for assisting shipping in and out of the docks. He also supervised the towing of barges out to sea after dredging operations and attended to the navigation buoys and crew changes on the Solway Light Ship.

He married Sarah Ann Connell, a native of Annan. They had two sons and four daughters. He was an enthusiastic member of the Bowling Club as well as a model maker.

He died suddenly, while working on his allotment, in October 1918. At his funeral, there were floral tributes from the Royal Antediluvian Order of Buffaloes, the crew of the 'Petrel' and one, in the shape of an anchor, from the harbour staff.

His younger son, Duncan, was unable to attend the funeral. He was, at the time, in a military hospital near Wigan, recovering from the effects of gas poisoning. His story is told in the next chapter.

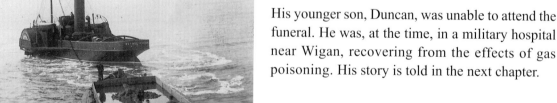

Left: *The tug 'Petrel' towing barges out to sea, after dredging operations in the docks.*

Capt. Chisholm on the bridge.

The 'Yarrow' (right) provided a twice-weekly service between Silloth and Dublin. Her crew (above) posed for the camera in 1912. The stewardess is Sarah Mahony Cunnigham, to her right is first Officer, William Kearney. We think the lad at the top of the ladder is Duncan Chisholm, Jnr who later became the ship's engineer. Captain Carnie was in charge.

The view of the inner dock (below) was taken in 1914. The barque 'Lota' is moored next to the flour mill. Visitors are watching as the 'Alya' arrives from Liverpool. The old Solway Light Ship can be seen moored at the far wall of the dock.

Annie Gibb

Annie Gibb opened her photographic studio, above Martin's shop, sometime around 1910. She ran it for the next 25 years. Tassels, the Carlisle photographers, had operated the studio for a few years before that. It is possible that Annie had worked as an assistant with them.

The entrance to Annie's studio can be seen on the extreme left of this picture. Note the large window on the first floor to allow the maximum natural light to fall on her customers.

At this time, it was very unusual for a woman to be involved in photography. It was virtually unknown for one to set up in business on their own account.

Annie was a remarkable woman. She must have developed and printed all her own photographic plates, sharing the darkroom where Sidney Martin produced the masters for his postcards.

She was born at Alnwick in Northumberland in 1874. Her father, Thomas Gibb, her brother, Harry Phelan, and her sister, Sadie, were all successful artists. All three exhibited their oils and water colours in galleries throughout northern England and Scotland. Annie never married and died, back home in Northumberland, in 1951.

'Otter Hunting on the Tweed' a typical work by Thomas Gibb, Annie's father.

These pages feature some of Annie's wonderful pictures of characters from the 1910 Silloth Carnival.

Look closely at this group – all the gentlemen are ladies!

The Happy Valley

David Fuller and his troupe of Merry Men and Maids.

One summer evening in 1901, three figures in pierrot costume wheeled a piano across Silloth green; they did not realise that they were establishing one of the town's 'Institutions'.

Several locals gathered to hear the performance, near the bank at the north end of the green which formed a natural auditorium. Three men – David Fuller, George Worthington and Arthur Court – entertained them with song, music and humour. The audience must have been impressed, because these entertainers were to give many more performances.

The site between a pine tree enclosure and North House became their home and was known as the Happy Valley. With swings and a seesaw nearby and chairs for the audience, the place became popular with the crowds who came to Silloth.

By 1908, there were nine in the troupe, still led by David Fuller, and a covered stage had been built with a changing room at the back.

The troupe became the subject of many picture postcards, making them quite famous.

A Very Fashionable Resort

Silloth Green, around 1910. The sea water baths can be seen in the distance. A small brass band is making its way along Criffel Street. The fashion parade is well underway.

As the new century dawned, Silloth was a very fashionable place to stay. The Aristocracy never arrived but the resort was immensely popular with the upper-middle classes; so was Allonby. These families would stay for several weeks during 'The Season'. They might rent an 'Apartment' in Silloth or a 'Villa' in Allonby. Others would choose to stay at the luxurious, modern Skinburness Hotel.

Every day, they would promenade along the sea front. The way a person dressed indicated their class and status in society. The upper class ladies who came to Silloth would change several times a day. Many would bring their own lady's maid to assist them in dressing. These servants stayed in the same accommodation as their employers.

Many of these well-to-do visitors would be wearing new and unusual fashions. These would be noted by the local ladies and copied by their dressmakers. The more prosperous local residents were very fashion conscious and quickly adopted the latest styles.

James Stronach was the main shipping broker for the port at Silloth. He would organise contacts between merchants and ship-owners, arrange for ships' supplies and their insurance. He also had a

James and Hanna Stronach with their children, Agnes, Stuart and John Arthur.

side-line in importing large quantities of slate from the mines in Wales. He lived with his family and one domestic servant. In their family portrait above Hannah Stronach is wearing the fashionable loose bodied blouse with the high collar and sleeves with fullness gathered into wristbands. Her tiny waist is emphasised by a broad belt. The boys are in sailor suits, a style popularised by the Royal Family. James is dressed as the perfect Edwardian gentleman with his high-buttoned waistcoat and watch chain. His separate starched collar is high and stiff and would have been attached to the shirt with a stud.

The ladies may also have patronised one of the new department stores which were just starting to appear in Carlisle and the other larger towns. Many of these also offered a mail order service.

Men's suits would be made-to-measure by one of the local tailors. There was Redmaynes in Wigton or Crones in Maryport. Crones employed seventeen tailors who worked in rooms under their shop in Senhouse Street.

A little further down the social scale, came the shopkeepers and the more prosperous farmers. Their clothing was less fussy and more practical. Improvements in manufacturing and transport made ready-to-wear clothes cheaper and more available. A good selection of these would be found at Maryport Co-op, which opened in 1900. It was a large store selling clothes, underwear and shoes as well as household goods. Customers there could become 'members' and, not only received a dividend, but might also pay for their goods in weekly instalments.

Miss Bookless from Allonby (above) is wearing her furs with a full length tailored dress and a rather strange hat. Both she and Mrs Stronach would have bought their clothes from their favourite fashion house or dressmaker. Some of these dressmakers travelled around the county by pony and trap. They took a hand sewing machine with them and often stayed at a customer's house for a week or two while they made and mended clothes for all the family.

Ben Bell (below) was the postmaster at Mawbray. He has taken his wife, Mary Ann, and sons Joseph, John and William to the photographers. Everybody is wearing their very best clothes. Ben was also a Methodist local preacher and a bit of a ladies man.

This group of ladies and gentlemen from Allonby are wearing their finery. The ladies have fashionably large hats, elaborately decorated with artificial flowers, frills, ostrich plumes and feathers. Large coiffures were needed to secure the hats with the aid of long, sharp-pointed hat pins.

Farmer Richard Littleton and his family about 1910; the children are (left to right) Mary (later Hurst), Rachel, Martha and John. They farmed at Skinburness.

Mary, John and Thomas Ostle were brothers and sister. None of them ever married.

David Over (above) is in his working clothes. He is standing outside his jewellers and watchmakers shop in Station Road, Silloth. His daughter, Annie is holding on tightly.

Young ladies, like the Littletons, wore their hair down until they were eighteen. Then they swept it up into one of the popular, full styles. Some ladies, with less abundant locks, used hair pieces and pads, known as rats, which were secured with hairpins to achieve the look. The Littleton girls may have made some of their own clothes. Sewing machines were becoming more affordable and, using paper patterns, made home dressmaking a cost effective option.

The Littletons seem to have been photographed in their farmyard. It was unusual for such family groups to be taken 'on location'. They are usually posed in the photographer's studio.

Perhaps there was a local photographer who travelled around the farms doing this sort of work. It might have been the same man who arrived unexpectedly and captured the Ostles of Cowgate in their working clothes!

Pictures of working men from this period are very rare; this one (below) shows a group of dockers at Silloth. They are pictured next to the pier, apparently engaged in salvaging the hull of the Scotsman, a coastal brigantine, wrecked in the Solway in February 1906.

Goodness knows where these fellows bought their clothes; they probably relied on the regular jumble sales organised by the local churches and chapels.

Perhaps readers recognise an ancestor in the group?

The 19th Hole

Golf was always one of Silloth's main leisure activities for both visitors and local people. The club had been formed in 1894. This was their original club house. It was purchased, second-hand from a tennis club in Dalston, near Carlisle. By the early 1900s, a fine new building had appeared by the first tee but the old hut remained in service for

some years. Eventually, the hut was replaced by a fine new extension to the club house.

The new premises included this fine 'Mixed' Dining Room. Ladies, of course, were not permitted in the main building's bar. The poster on the wall is dated 1912.

A fast Carr

Theodore Carr with brother Bertram aboard.

Theodore Carr was a mechanical whizz-kid. He made many innovations in his family's biscuit and flour business. In 1896, with some help from a Carlisle cycle dealer, he made himself a motor car. It was the first to be seen on the streets of Carlisle or Silloth.

It was a petrol driven three-wheeler which generated terrifying clouds of steam. Theodore lived in Dalston, a few miles outside Carlisle, from where he drove to work each morning. He also made regular trips to the coast

.
In May 1900, he was summoned to appear before Wigton Magistrates for exceeding the speed limit, then 12 miles per hour, in Abbeytown. P.C. Lace testified that he was standing at Swinsty crossroads, when he saw the car coming over the railway bridge. There were three children playing on the roadside and he signalled the driver to stop. When Theodore ignored him, he jumped onto the fence and timed the vehicle between the junction and the next railway bridge at the other side of the village, one mile away. The distance was covered in two minutes.

Another witness, Johnston Mattinson, a joiner, said he had been very frightened and thought it a miracle that there hadn't been an accident. Theodore denied going at anything like the 35mph claimed by the police. He said, "If I had been endangering the lives of the inhabitants, I should have thought the constable would have warned me". "He couldn't catch you", replied Supt. Ross who was conducting the prosecution.

Theodore was fined £1, plus costs. He thanked the bench and said he would be glad to give any of their Worships a ride on the machine after the court rose. They could then test its powers of speed and safety for themselves.

Two years later, Theodore was again accused of speeding. On this occasion, he was driving along the coast at Beckfoot. A local man, Robert Armstrong, was also on the road, going in the opposite direction, with his family in a pony and trap. He got the others out of the cart when he saw the car coming and waved at the driver to stop. He was ignored and the pony took fright, jumping around wildly. This time Theodore was fined a total of £6 plus costs.

The Railways

Many writers portray Edwardian railways as a dream world of Railway Children and country stations like Adlestrop. As far as the locals were concerned, the local lines were more like a nightmare!

The services were run by three separate companies with no co-ordination between them. In 1910 the Maryport & Carlisle Railway offered its passengers a special week-end return to Silloth which involved them using trains operated by all three companies. On Friday and Saturday only, trippers could leave Wigton at 1.30pm. They then had to wait three-quarters of an hour at Brayton, just outside Aspatria, for the 2.27 Special, operated by the Caledonian Railway, to Abbey Junction. Here they had to change again, to a North British Railway train arriving in Silloth at 2.57. Almost one-and-a-half hours to cover a distance of nine miles as the crow flies!

A real problem arose on Monday morning when they wanted to get home and there was no 'Special'. They had to catch the 8.00am from Silloth. With two changes, this would get them home to Wigton at 9.20 – a bit late for work! If they missed that train the next one, at 10.55, had no connections and they wouldn't get back until 3.25 in the afternoon.

The North British Railway, which operated the line from Carlisle to Silloth, seems to have lost interest in the branch after the Settle-Carlisle line opened in 1876. By1910, there were only four trains on weekdays in each direction. On Thursdays

and Saturdays there was an extra '*express*' service from Carlisle to Silloth but even this took forty-five minutes to cover the twenty two and a half miles of track!

The timings were not particularly convenient. It would have been difficult for a mill worker from Carlisle to fit in a day-trip. In those days he would only have had Saturday afternoon and Sunday off work. The express train left the city at 11.45am – before his finishing time. The next, at two o'clock would give him less than five hours at the seaside before catching the last train home at 7.50pm. There were no trains at all on a Sunday.

It was not only seaside trippers who found the service poor. In September 1905, the Holm Cultram Council sent a petition to the Board of Trade, asking them to compel the NBR to provide a better service. Francis Grainger, the chairman, said it was the worst served line in Cumberland – perhaps in the whole North of England. He thought that "insufficient railway accommodation was retarding Silloth's progress as a holiday resort."

He explained that, when local farmers purchased cattle in Carlisle, they were sent straight to Silloth and then shunted back to Abbeytown. One councillor thought it might be quicker to send them to Kirtlebridge in Scotland and bring them back over the Solway viaduct! He suggested local farmers should boycott the line altogether.

Bromfield Station

Note the magnificent floral displays; the staff had plenty of time to tend them, there were only three trains a day in each direction!

From here the trains ran to Bowness-on-Solway and then on to a viaduct over the Solway to Annan in Scotland.

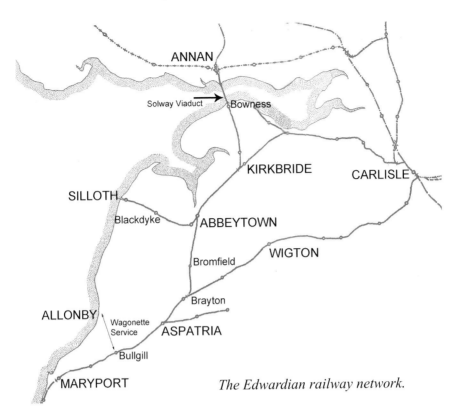

The Edwardian railway network.

Silloth station with a train approaching from Carlisle

The railway yard at Silloth.

Kirkbride Station

Abbeytown Station

Allonby

Allonby around 1900. The old cast-iron bridge was destroyed when a traction engine fell through it in 1905.

The village was always a popular place for summer holidays and most families let one or two of their rooms to visitors during the season. The *Carlisle Journal* often published a list of current holiday makers. The vast majority were local people, many from the Keswick and Cockermouth areas. There were some from further afield; they came from the South of Scotland, Lancashire and Tyneside, there were even families from London and Liskeard in Devon!

Cricket matches took place regularly on the green throughout the Edwardian years. The scorecard shows the village team beating Silloth by 12 runs. Amos Bookless was Allonby's demon bowler taking five wickets, but being out for a duck when he came in to bat for them at number ten. John Tocher, the postman, made up for this, scoring a magnificent thirty-one, only being caught on the last ball of the match.

SILLOTH.		ALLONBY.	
Humble, b Bookless	4	Tocher, c Dodd, b Richards	33
Bell, c Bunting, b Bookless	0	Bunting, c Moore, b Richards	2
Moore, b Bookless	8	Faulder, b Richards	0
Dodd, b Hampson	7	Hampson, b H'mble	3
Pape, c Carruthers, b Bunting	15	Crozier, c Dodd, b Richards	25
Smith, b Bunting	7	Croft, c Bell, b Richards	7
Richards, c Tocher, b Bookless	6	Hodgs'n, b Rich'rds	0
Batey, b Bunting	3	Carruthers, c Hum- Metcalfe, b Rich'rds	1
Lawson, c and b Bookless	4	Bookless, c Pape, b Beaty	0
Mattinson, not out	0	Williamson, not out	0
Cameron, c Crozi'r, b Bunting	1		
Extras	7	Extras	3
Total	62	Total	74

Amos Bookless, stage designer and cricketer.

In April 1909, early visitors and local people alike were entranced by the 'Living Waxworks' show presented in the Church Hall. The event was organised by Nellie Hodgson, who appeared as 'Mrs Jarley' the waxworks proprietor and recited 'autogeographies' of all the exhibits complete with many other malapropisms. She was assisted by Amos Bookless who had also, at his own expense, produced the elaborate and beautiful scenery for the occasion.

Mr Steele from Bowscale Farm appeared as John Peel. James Twentyman doubled-up as both a Chinese Giant and an American Scarecrow. Miss Ena Shadwick took the part of Grace Darling and Miss S. Harrison was, mysteriously, billed as an Old-fashioned Sewing Machine!

Christopher Columbus, Simple Simon, Red Riding Hood, Britannia and a Cruel Nursemaid also appeared. Mrs Alma Maria Blackstock of the village Fancy Goods Store was at the piano. The press reported that "most of those who took part were making almost, if not quite, their first appearance on stage. The usual performers were taking a rest and appearing in the audience".

Alma Blackstock, pianist at her day job.

John and Ann Hodgson (left) lived at Bank House. John acted as bailiff for the Lords of the Manor, Ann let rooms to visitors.

Their daughters, Margaret and Agnes, both took part in the 'Living Waxworks' show.

Margaret appeared as 'Matilda Muggins, Queen of the Gipsies' while Agnes took the role of a Lancashire Lass.

1906 had been a year of new facilities. The bridge lost in the previous year was rebuilt. A new church hall was built and Allonby got its first bank. The branch of the York City and County bank was opened in a house belonging to Mr. Colin Ravell, following alterations.

Also, on February 16th that year, Allonby was declared a parish in its own right, distinct from Bromfield, of which it had previously been part.

Opening of the village hall.

The ship breakers of Allonby

Vessels await dismantling at Allonby. About 1908.

At the beginning of the twentieth century, Allonby was home to a surprising business – the dismantling of ships.

The activity had begun in the 1880s but reached its height in the late 1890s and early 1900s, when several local men and boys were employed.

The operation was the idea of Captain John Twentyman, an Allonby Mariner born in 1839. His family had been involved with the sea there for years before. He knew the shipping business and

Some ships recycled at Allonby.....		
Brigantine	'Old Adventure'	119 tons
Ship	'Falcon'	794 tons
Brigantine	'Puella'	134 tons
	'Defiance'	204 tons
	'Hippolyte'	200 tons
Schooner	'Onyx'	197 tons
Schooner	'Sac-a-farine'	150 tons
Schooner	'Mary Connick'	163 tons
Brigantine	'Orion'	116 tons
Barque	'Helios'	437 tons
Barque	'Valborg'	760 tons
Barque	'Belle Flower'	360 tons
Ship	'Prince Victor'	1,160 tons
Barque	'Hilda'	1,137 tons

The hull of the 'Esther', one of the last of the Allonby fishing wherries, lies on the beach prior to being broken up. Note the size of the hull compared to the figures in the foreground.

had access to the information necessary to purchase vessels. He bought ships that came onto the market, usually ones which had reached the end of useful career. After having their masts and loose fittings removed, he arranged for them to be towed up to Allonby Bay on high tides. They would come to rest high on the beach where dismantling could take place. All the ships were made of wood with some metal fittings. At the time, iron and steel hulled vessels were taking over and an increasing number of wooden ships were being disposed of. John went into partnership with his relation, John Dickson. John came from Caerlaverock, across the Solway, near Dumfries. His sister Jane had married James Twentyman, also a mariner, in 1874. After moving to Allonby in the 1870s, Dickson worked first as a fisherman, and later as a shopkeeper, before doing the shipbreaking. In 1898 the family links were increased when he married Elizabeth Ann Twentyman, his business partner's eldest daughter. Also involved in the business were John Twentyman's two nephews, William and James, and the 1901 census shows two other villagers, William Messenger and Stephen Hodgson, working for him. Others helped on a casual basis.

The business was really a timber merchant; it was the value of the wood which was the basis of the operation. Ships were made of good strong timber and this was a quality building material which would last. A variety of woods including teak, oak and pine were salvaged and sold on for a variety of uses. Some of the ships were British and some foreign. Several, such as the 'Sac a Farine' and 'Mary Connick', had been regular visitors to Solway ports. Most of the vessels were taken into Mayport prior to beaching, but two, the 'Hilda' and the 'Prince Victor' had their masts and gear removed at Silloth.

The ships were taken apart using hand tools and the wood was taken away in large carts pulled by two strong horses. Capt. Twentyman had a workshop nearby where the wood was sawn up and stored ready for sale. This timber found a variety of uses: pit props, roof beams, gates, fences and fuel. Many buildings on the Solway Plain put up or repaired in the early twentieth century contain wood from vessels broken up at Allonby.

The work came to an end around 1912. Capt. Twentyman was now in his 70s, and he passed away not long after, in 1915. The other men were young enough to continue but gave it up, probably due to the supply of wooden ships being limited by now, and their lacking the resources to deal in metal hulks.

For many years after, figureheads and other ship decoration could be found in houses and gardens around the village, reminders of the ships which ended their lives at Allonby.

An invoice for wood supplied

Sir Walter Scott
Civil Engineer, 1st Baronet of Beauclere

Walter Scott was born in 1826 at the old Wheatsheaf Inn in Abbeytown.

He served his apprenticeship as a mason and then found work with the railway company. This took him to Newcastle-on-Tyne where, in 1849, he established his own business as a builder and contractor.

His company were responsible for several important buildings in Newcastle-on-Tyne. These included major hotels, the Tyne Theatre and the portico at Newcastle Central Station. Locally, Scott's company were responsible for building the new docks at Silloth which opened in 1885. The hydraulic system there was designed and installed by another famous engineer based in Newcastle – Lord Armstrong.

Scott specialised in large-scale contracts including railway construction and built the first deep underground 'tube' railway in London working alongside its engineer, James Greathead. The City and South London Railway was opened in November 1890 by the Prince of Wales. It ran from King William Street, under the Thames, to Stockwell.

At first, it used a system of cable haulage but this was soon abandoned and replaced by electric traction. The station at King William Street and the tunnels under the Thames closed in 1900 but the station re-opened in 1940 and was used as an air-raid shelter.

Scott was engaged to build a printing factory for the Tyne Publishing Company, but the company failed in January 1882. Although Scott had no experience in printing or publishing, he took over the business in lieu of payment for the factory. He appointed David Gordon, a bookbinder, as general manager and the business prospered. The company was the first to publish Ibsen in English.

Scott's business interests widened and, before he died, he had a seat on the boards of at least eighteen companies including steelworks, coalmines and shipyards. He was a councillor and JP for Northumberland. He was created a Baronet in the king's birthday honours for 1907.

Sir Walter's first wife died in 1890. He erected the magnificent East Window of Holm Cultram Abbey Church in her memory. He was later remarried to a widow, Helen Meikle.

He died, while on holiday, at Menton in France during April 1910. He left just over £1,424,000; one of only fifteen true self-made millionaires in Britain before 1939. His company continued to build tube railways into the 1920s.

His own memorial at Abbeytown was the restored oak ceiling in the Abbey which, sadly, was completely destroyed in the fire of 2006.

The New Dock at Silloth under construction in 1885. Note the steam-powered crane to the right of the railway wagons.

Edwardian Abbeytown

The school with its unfenced playground.

The 'Straits'. These long demolished buildings stood on the road leading to the abbey which can just be seen in the distance. The building with the steps was known as 'the old boardroom'.

Above: *The main street.*

Right: *The Parish Church, all that remains of the 12th century Cistercian monastery which gave the village its name.*

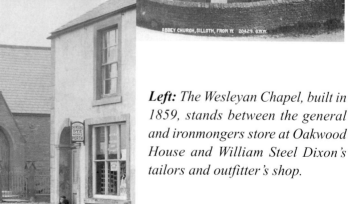

Left: *The Wesleyan Chapel, built in 1859, stands between the general and ironmongers store at Oakwood House and William Steel Dixon's tailors and outfitter's shop.*

CHAPTER TWO

1914 – 1918, The First World War

Silloth Town Band leads the local Artillery Volunteers along Eden Street.

Britain declared war on 4th August 1914 – right in the middle of the tourist season in Allonby and Silloth. The hotels and boarding houses were packed with visitors.

At first, there was little disruption to the local community although a detachment of Marines arrived at Silloth within a week. Their orders were to guard the 'Battery' – the weapons proving range operated by Armstrong-Whitworth of Newcastle.

By the end of August, special constables had been sworn-in at Silloth and Abbeytown. A meeting for this purpose was also called at Holme St Cuthberts – but nobody turned up. A passenger from Dublin was arrested when he disembarked from the 'Yarrow' and accused of being a German spy. He was quickly released without charge. There was panic right along the coast when an aeroplane was sighted. A large number of refugees from the fighting in Belgium arrived in Britain and several families were accommodated in Allonby and Silloth.

At the Hydro Hotel in Silloth, the proprietor, Charles Hawkins, discovered two cash boxes, an overcoat and a chisel had been stolen. His waiter, Friedrich Wolfojoinej Oderich, and his wife, Lily, the cook, were arrested after a chase through Gale Woods at Abbeytown. They were charged with the theft and also of failing to register as enemy aliens.

In court, Charles Hawkins explained that officials from the labour exchange in Carlisle had asked him to give Lily a job as she was destitute and assured him she was Swiss. He took pity on her husband who was also homeless and gave him work too. Friedrich got twelve months' hard labour and Lily one month.

These trivial incidents, all reported in the local papers, give the impression that the war was having little real effect on the local area. Indeed, throughout the whole duration, there were few disruptions to life in the local communities. A gunnery school and firing range were established at Skinburness but this was the only military presence in the area.

It was to be events far away, overseas, that were to have a tragic and devastating effect on many local families.

29

Gallipoli

On June 4th, 1915, a group of Silloth lads came ashore at Gallipoli. They were all in the Royal Naval Division, part of the Royal Naval Volunteer Reserve which had been placed under army command at the behest of Winston Churchill.

Within two days, three of them were dead. Another died two weeks later, probably from wounds received earlier and a fifth died, during August, at a military hospital in Alexandria. Several others were badly wounded.

The men were part of a large force, sent to relieve the stalemate which had developed between the allied armies and the defending Turkish forces on the peninsula. Both sides were entrenched and under heavy shelling. Despite the complete failure of their previous attempts, the British generals planned a new assault against the Turkish lines. This was to take place on June 4th and later became known as The Third Battle of Krihia. This was the action in which the Silloth men were involved.

The men landed at Sulva Bay and fought their way over a dried-up salt lake toward the Turkish lines. Under cover of a heavy naval bombardment, the troops dug into trenches. When the shelling ended, they charged "over the top" into a murderous hail of artillery from the Turkish positions.

On the left flank, hundreds of Lancashire Fusiliers and Sheiks were mown down. On the right flank the three battalions of RND men made it to the enemy lines but, with only 330 men and 20 officers left, were forced to withdraw to their original trenches.

In gaining less than a mile of territory, the allies had suffered 6,500 casualties. Turkish losses were estimated at 9,000. Fighting continued all through the summer and autumn but no real gains were ever made. The last men were evacuated on December 20th.

The Gallipoli Peninsula, 1915

In 1914, Turkey was still part of the Ottoman Empire which had joined the war on the Germans' side.

The main landings at Gallipoli had taken place in April. British forces occupied the southern tip of the peninsula and the Australian and New Zealand army landed further north, at what was to become known as Anzac Cove. Both groups suffered heavy casualties and became pinned down in their trenches by the defending forces.

The original plan had been for the two armies to join up and occupy the whole peninsula. This would have given the Allies control of the shipping lanes through The Dardanelles to Constantinople and the Black Sea.

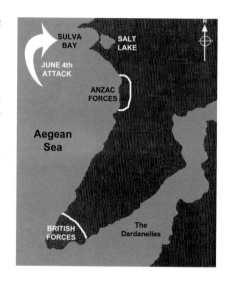

In June, reinforcements were sent involving over 75,000 men including 10,000 members of the Royal Naval Division.

Tom Hunter of Langrigg writes home . . .

. . . The 4th of June was my unlucky day. The great bombardment began at 11am and, you can take it from me, it was a bombardment. I shall never forget it as long as I live. The French 75s (of which, no doubt, you will have read) were booming all day and our batteries were busy; also some battleships were firing from the sea. The idea of it all was to try and capture the strong position of the Turks on a hill named Achi-Baba.

This hill is a very great stronghold but, I'll bet, there weren't many Turks alive that day, as the hill was a complete mass of smoke caused by the bursting shells. We got the order to stand by at 11am and we moved off about 1pm. When we got so far up, the bullets started to whizz round us like peas and we lost a few men.

As we were going up, we met the wounded coming down and I saw some sights that day I shall never forget. Nobody knows what war is until they have had a taste. The Collingwood Battalion were nearly wiped out, poor chaps. They made a bayonet charge under a murderous fire of rifles and machine guns, also of shrapnel.

The Turks were using an explosive bullet, and a Maryport chap had one in his arm. It went into his arm and exploded, breaking his arm and making an awful hole. He said there was one chap had both legs blown off, and he was conscious for an hour; but I mustn't tell you the horrors of war until I come home.

Well, we plodded away and, at last, got into the trenches, where we were going to re-enforce the firing line and make another charge, but I had the luck to get one through the neck about 8pm. It was a funny feeling, I can tell you. It was a good job it wasn't an explosive bullet. I had quick attention and our officer took me down to the first field dressing station. From there, I was helped along by ambulance men and, finally, taken in a van to the base on the shore. I stayed there all night and next morning was taken to [CENSORED]. We left on Sunday, 6th June and arrived at Malta on the 9th.

I was taken to the Royal Naval Hospital and stayed there until the 14th when I was transferred to H.M.S. [CENSORED] which is really a barracks and Convalescent Home. I am getting on fine and they say we are going to Alexandria from here, so I won't be in the firing line for a while yet. If we once get the hill Achi-Baba, the Turks' number is up.

Don't you worry about me, as I seem to know I am coming through all right. I don't profess to be a great Christian but, I can tell you, I turned myself a bit when I got amongst the shells and bullets, and I said my prayers every night in the dug-outs.

When I got shot, I thought I was gone and I just murmured to myself 'O Lord, take me to your heavenly home'. He spared me and, I am sure, he will spare me to come back to home and you. Kindly remember me to all in the district. I am in the best of health and spirits and all I want is for you not to worry about me.

This letter was published in the *Carlisle Journal* on June 29th, 1915.

Three men who came home . . . .

Duncan Chisholm

Duncan had just turned twenty when he enlisted in the RND. His family background suited him to a life at sea; his father was captain of the Silloth tug. He took part in the landings at Sulva Bay and his name appeared in the casualty lists as 'Missing' after the action.

He must have survived somehow as, four years later, he was in action again on the front line in France where he was gassed in a German attack. He was brought back to England where he spent some time in hospital recovering.

After the war he became second engineer on the S.S. 'Assaroe', which sailed regularly between Silloth and Dublin. When this service was suspended, in 1943, he went to work at Carr's Mill.

He was a familiar figure in the town, along with his wife, Jessie, but always suffered from problems with his chest due to the gassing.

William Gibson Richardson

William lived at Blitterlees with his wife, Sarah Jane, always known as 'Tadie' He was a merchant seaman, serving on the S.S. 'Albatross'. He was a member of the Royal Navy Volunteer Reserve and was awarded their long service medal.

William saw action at Gallipoli but his family believe that he didn't actually take part in the landings. He served on one of the ships which were used as troop transport and hospital ships. After the war, he worked on Silloth Docks and often assisted with the unloading of Irish cattle at the lairage.

William and Sarah had one girl and three boys. All the boys went to sea. The two eldest, James and John, are in the photograph. William's brother, Petty Officer Thomas Richardson, was in the Royal Navy. He served aboard H.M.S. 'Formidable' and lost his life in the early hours of New Year's Day, 1915 when she was torpedoed by a U-boat in the English Channel.

. . . .

And those who didn't . . . .

A.B. Samuel Borthwick, R.N.D.
(Collingwood Battalion)
Killed in action, 4th June 1915, aged 20.
A labourer, son of John and Martha Borthwick, 24, Wampool Street.

A.B. Stanley Gordon Brown, R.N.D.
(Hawke Battalion)
Killed in action, 19th June 1915, aged 24.
Articled to John Errington, Solicitor, Carlisle. His mother lived in Wiggonby.

A.B. Joseph Johnston, R.N.D.
(Collingwood Battalion)
Died of wounds 4th June 1915 in Royal Navy Field Ambulance Station, aged 24.
A barber, son of Joseph Johnston, 1 Raglan Court.
"a popular young man and a footballer"

A.B. Edgar Sisson Swan, R.N.D.
(Collingwood Battalion)

Died of wounds aboard Hospital Ship 'Southland' 6th June 1915, aged 17
Son of Mr and Mrs Andrew D. Swan, 3 Beaconsfield Terrace.
"a familiar figure on golf course as caddy and player".

Petty Officer John Jefferson Underwood, R.N.D. (Anson Battalion)
Died of Enteric Fever in 17th General Hospital, Alexandria 19th August 1915, aged 33.
A ship's stoker. Lived with his wife at Prospect Place, West Silloth.

Thomas Stanwix, D.C.M.
Thomas, a farm lad from Blitterlees, enlisted in the Royal Naval Division in November 1914.
He made it through the early stages of the Gallipoli landings but, in August 1915, suffered "severe, multiple shell wounds in the forearm, nose and thigh". He was taken to hospital in Malta and, eventually, back to the Royal Naval Hospital in Portland.
After recovering from his wounds, in November 1916, he was in action again on the western front. Thomas was again wounded in May 1918. He was then promoted and became involved in the logistics of supplying the front-line troops.
He was awarded the Distinguished Conduct Medal. The citation states "This man has, on three occasions shown the most daring devotion to duty while under shell fire; twice, remaining at his post when wounded".
Thomas never talked much about his experiences but often recalled that, when he returned home, he had to undress and bath in the byre to get rid of the lice and mud before he went into the house.

Cannon Walker and Family

*Cannon Walker with his sons,
(left to right) Edward, Cuthbert and William.*

Cannon Robert Walker was vicar of St Pauls, Causewayhead from 1898 until 1936. He had three sons, all of whom distinguished themselves during the First World War.

Lieut. (Reverend) Edward Walker served in France as a chaplain and interpreter with the Labour Corps.

Lt. Col. William Keating Walker, DSO and bar, MC, CdeG (France) known as 'Tiny', had emigrated to Canada, a few years before the war. He enlisted in August 1914 and, in November, received a commission in the Royal Canadian Dragoons.

Between 1915 and 1916, he was wounded twice in France and, in May 1918, was appointed as Commanding Officer of the First Canadian Motor Machine Gun Brigade, just as a major German offensive began. The brigade was involved in fighting at Bois Moreuil and held over 2,500 yards of the front line. For his part in this action, William received the DSO.

In November 1918, the Canadian forces entered Mons and held a Victory Parade with Walker's brigade in a leading role. The following year the king presented him with a bar to his DSO at Buckingham Palace.

On his return to England, William Walker launched a public appeal to purchase new colours for the Motor Machine Gun Brigade. On March 23rd 1919, the Mayor of Carlisle presented these to the regiment on the town hall steps. William retired from the Canadian Forces in 1930.

Vehicles of the Canadian Motor Machine Brigade

Presentation of the new colours at Carlisle. Lt. Col. Walker is standing to the left of the table.

Lt. Col. Cuthbert H. "Johnnie" Walker, MC, was Cannon Walker's youngest son. In October 1914, aged 19, he joined the 11th Battalion of the Border Regiment, the 'Lonsdales', as a second lieutenant.

He left for France a year later and was severely wounded at Authuille Wood during Battle of the Somme, in July 1916. He was awarded the Military Cross for his gallantry there. He was out of action for several months but re-joined the regiment and fought with them until July 1917 when he was again badly wounded.

After the war, Cuthbert Walker became a regular soldier, serving in Ireland, Malta, Aden, India and Palestine. During the Second World War, he acted as commanding officer of the Border Regiment's 'Home Detail' which was responsible for the defence of East Anglia. He retired from the regular army in 1946 and then became the secretary of the Cumberland and Westmorland Territorial Army and Air Force Association. He died in 1949.

The Military Cross.

The Lonsdales

Lord Lonsdale formed the 11th Battalion of the Border Regiment in September 1914. The war office gave him permission to attach his own name to them. They were one of the numerous 'Pals Battalions' formed on the outbreak of war. The men all came from Carlisle and the surrounding towns and villages.

The officers of the Lonsdale Battalion.

Cuthbert Walker is second from the right on the third row back.
*Sixth from the left, on the same row is **Lt. William Sibson Barnes . . .***

. . . **William Sibson Barnes** was born at Mawbray House Farm in 1892. His parents, William and Mary, died within a few months of each other in 1900 and he then went to live with the Rev John Bardsley and his family at Holme St Cuthbert's vicarage.

After leaving Holme St Cuthbert's School, William served his articles as a surveyor at the Wigton Rural District Council. In 1913, he emigrated to Canada and enlisted there on the outbreak of war. He returned to England with the first contingent of Canadian soldiers to arrive and quickly obtained a commission in the Lonsdale Battalion of the Border Regiment. He became engaged to Miss Vida Maxwell of Norfolk Road, Carlisle whose father was proprietor of the Solway Chemical works in Silloth.

Lt. Barnes was soon posted to France. By the spring of 1916, he was on the front line. The Allies were planning a major offensive for the summer – what we now know as The Battle of the Somme. The Lonsdales were to play a major part in the action.

In May, Lt. Barnes was chosen to lead a reconnaissance mission into the German trenches. All the men for this mission were to be volunteers. It is hardly surprising that one of those who came forward was one of the lieutenant's old schoolmates, Thomas Richardson. Thomas was twenty-three years old. His parents, Joseph and Elizabeth Richardson, lived in Mawbray where Joseph worked as a hired man.

Lt. Barnes spent three weeks training his men. They practised bomb-throwing and had two hours of physical training each day. They also received instruction on conducting prisoners and carrying the wounded.

On the morning of June 5th, the men received orders that the raid was to be carried out that night. At 9 pm, they moved up to the front and, at 10 0'clock went "over the top" with revolvers, torches, compasses and blackened faces.

During the first stages of the attack, Private Richardson was wounded. Despite this, he carried on and entered the German trench, helping the other men in the capture of eleven prisoners, and then struggled back to the British trenches. Here,

Lt. William Sibson Barnes

Private Thomas Richardson M.M.

he must have collapsed and been taken to the field hospital.

Lieutenant Barnes also made it back to the British line but then, according to the account of another of the soldiers, returned to No Man's Land to retrieve his revolver, which he had dropped during the action. A German sniper saw him and shot him dead with a single bullet to the chest.

In all, seven members of the battalion died during the raid and twenty-seven were wounded. Eleven German prisoners were taken and it was estimated that a further twenty-five enemy soldiers had been killed.

The raid was considered a great success. The Battalion's C.O., Colonel Machell, wrote: "the success of the enterprise was due to the great care that Lt. Barnes took in training and his leadership up to the end was most splendid."

Four days later, Private Thomas Richardson died from his wounds. For his gallantry, while under fire and wounded, he was awarded the Military Medal.

The award was confirmed in the London Gazette of 10th August, 1916. His captain wrote to the family: "No man ever proved worthier of the honour."

On an early summer Sunday in 1916, a memorial service for both men was held at Holme St Cuthbert's church. It must have been a very sad occasion for the Rev Bardsley who conducted the service and his daughter who was the organist. They would have had many memories of the years William Barnes had spent living with them in the vicarage. The vicar must also have known Thomas Richardson as he was a regular visitor to the school.

The Richardsons were Methodists and, the following Sunday, yet another memorial service was held, this time at their chapel in Mawbray. It was conducted by a local preacher, Charles Hawkins, proprietor of the Silloth Hydro.

Thomas Richardson's brother, Will, and his grand-nephew, Robert, farmed at Newtown until 2003.

Silloth's secret weapons

Silloth battery.

A single line from the goods yard at Silloth headed south past the convalescent home and off into the sand hills of Blitterlees banks. After about a mile, the line ended, at a large compound containing several buildings and a large gantry crane. Signs warned the public to stay away from this curious facility, and what went on within the strong timber palisade fence was indeed intended to be secret; this was a high level military establishment.

In 1883, correspondence began between the North British Railway and the Newcastle firm of William Armstrong & Co.. Armstrong manufactured, among other things, heavy artillery and was seeking a place to test such products. A coastal site, where weapons could be fired out to sea, was sought and negotiations led to Armstrongs being allowed to set up their firing range. That was in 1886 but The Battery, as it became known, remained there well into the twentieth century.

Guns of various types and sizes were carried by rail from the factory at Elswick on the Tyne across to Silloth, often on specially designed rolling stock, covered by thick tarpaulins to hide the contents.

Once at the site, the wagons were shunted under a gantry crane which lifted each piece off and moved a few yards to the gun mounting places where the weapons would be fixed into position and test fired. Nearby were stores where shells and gunpowder were kept.

Although there was high security on the area, it was no secret what was going on. – People could hear the sounds of the gunfire miles away. On occasion, red warning flags were flown and signals placed to warn mariners, as all guns were aimed out into the Solway. Firing was done at low tide in order to avoid blowing up any passing vessels which may not have been aware of the range. After the tests, men from the site with a horse drawn wagon picked up the empty shell cartridges from the shore.

Armstrongs employed a full time site caretaker, who lived in a cottage in one corner of the compound. The site's first caretaker was Jabez Ault. He lived there with Ellen and their children until he died in 1910. His role was then taken by Walter Accleton who lived there, with his wife, until the site closed in 1928.

The house was sold but remained home to several families over the following years:

1930 Fred & Jane Render

1940 John Robinson and family

1945 Clarence Edmondson and family

1950 Gladys Borrows and family

1955 Josephine Latimer

The place was abandoned by the late 1950s and became a favourite haunt of children who enjoyed playing among its walls.

The Home Front

Silloth's old sea wall and the pavilion beyond North House where the Coronets performed.

During the early years of the war, things carried on much as normal. At Silloth, the Pierrots continued to perform and were joined by another concert party. A.C. Astor's Coronets performed in a specially constructed enclosure further along the sea front.

A.C. Astor was the stage name of Thomas Ferguson. He was born in Carlisle, but moved to Silloth with his family when his father set up there as a plumber. He joined David Fuller's troupe but soon left to start what proved to be a very successful show business career. He ran concert parties in several resorts, performed as a ventriloquist on the music halls and finally, became proprietor of Her Majesty's Theatre in Carlisle.

The Coronets on stage

In 1914, Mr Astor gave a picture show in the Oddfellows Hall at Silloth. This featured shots of the Lonsdale Battalion at work and play. The press reported that 'A number of local youths could easily be recognised on the screen and the item evoked loud applause'.

During Carlisle Race Week, David Fuller's troupe offered a special attraction. Mr Norman Donald, a popular performer from previous years, appeared in the uniform of the London Scottish of which he was a member. He performed his own composition, a recruiting song 'with a very catchy chorus, now on the tongues of all and sundry' – it went:

There's a first battalion fighting at the front,
There's a second battalion ready to bear the brunt,
There's a third battalion filling,
Forming up and drilling,
And every man should be willing to fight
Against the German sin.
Men, it's never too late to mend, maybe you've heard,
We want a couple of hundred men to fill the third.
So, hurry up, boys, and don't be slow
And help us crush the German foe
And march with the London Scottish to Berlin.

David Fuller's Pierrots

As the war progressed, the locals did begin to feel its effects at home. Conscription, for single men aged between 18 and 41, was introduced in 1916. There were exemptions for those in essential war time employment. Local tribunals assessed who qualified and most farmers applied to exempt their sons and labourers from the call-up. At the same time, a national campaign was launched to encourage women to volunteer for farm work.

Reports in the local papers suggest that these tribunals adopted a pretty hard line with the farmers. Joseph Jefferson of Home Farm, Langrigg applied

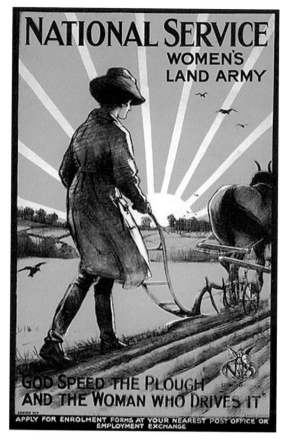

NATIONAL SERVICE WOMEN'S LAND ARMY

"GOD SPEED THE PLOUGH AND THE WOMAN WHO DRIVES IT"

APPLY FOR ENROLMENT FORMS AT YOUR NEAREST POST OFFICE OR EMPLOYMENT EXCHANGE

In May 1915, the Border Regiment held a recruiting campaign around the towns and villages of the Solway Plain. The top picture shows the party at Drumburgh. The lower photograph was taken at Mawbray. The Wigton Advertiser's report on the occasion says: "At Mawbray an elderly woman, a Mrs Armstrong, came forward and stated she had three sons in the army, one of whom is at present amongst the wounded in Woolwich hospital." This must have been 'Postie' Mary Armstrong who delivered the letters around the village. She was also to lose her grandson, Joseph William Armstrong, who was killed in action in April 1917.

for the exemption of his labourer, Isaac Elliot Fell Benn. The Military Representative on the tribunal told Jefferson to get women to do the work instead. He replied "Women will do a lot forking hay, won't they - how would you like to send your missus to fork hay?"

In another case, later the same day, Robert Shanks of Aigle Gill, applied for the exemption of his two labourers, Park and Muncaster. There was a government scheme which found work for refugees on farms. Shanks said he had tried to get two Danes in place of the men but the government had sent only one. Rev. W. Jefferson, a member of the panel asked where the Danes came from. "Denmark!" replied Shanks. Park and Muncaster were ordered to join the army.

Jonathan Strong of Drumleaning, near Wigton served on one of these tribunals. In June 1916, he addressed a meeting of local farmers and told them that there had been a good response to the appeal for women workers but he was "very sanguine" as to its success. He knew many farmers did not favour the idea but the time was coming when they would be glad to avail themselves of the women.

Mr Thompson of Cockbridge told the meeting it was Tommy-rot to say that women would not be able to do farm work. In munitions, women did not do equal work with the men but they did double. He asked what means were being taken to enable farmers to get at this reservoir of women labour which seemed to be full. What was to be done in the villages?

Miss La Mothe, an agricultural adviser to the Board of Trade, told him that, in every village, there was a registrar whose name could be seen in post offices. She hoped farmers who required women workers would apply to the registrar so that they could know where places were available.

Women at work in the munitions factory at Gretna.

Despite all these good intentions, it is difficult to find any evidence of women actually taking up jobs with local farmers. Many local girls may have found better paid work in the large munitions factories which had been built in Gretna and Carlisle. Many others were involved in nursing at both the large hospitals in Carlisle and, locally, in Silloth Convalescent Home.

Here many convalescent soldiers had been admitted as well as munitions workers from all parts of the region. In November 1917, a local lady wrote to Dr Barnes at the Convalescent Home about "the alleged unsatisfactory state of affairs that existed because Gretna girl ammunition workers were being admitted at the same time as soldiers". No more soldiers were to be accepted until the matter was settled. Finally, it was decided to continue to admit soldiers but no more girls from Gretna. Bad luck on the soldiers!

Mrs Jefferson from Edderside nursed at the Cumberland Infirmary in Carlisle.

Producing Cordite, known locally as the Devil's Porridge.

By 1917, supplies of food, especially wheat, were being badly disrupted by the German U-boat patrols. Local Food Committees were set up; they had the power to fix local prices for basic foodstuffs and to ensure their fair distribution.

In January 1918, the Holm Cultram Food Committee invited the local butchers to attend a meeting in the Cocoa House at Silloth. They agreed that all butchers shops in the area would close on Tuesday and Wednesday each week and that, on those days, no butchers' carts were to travel the rural areas.

The introduction of these 'Meatless Days' led to another meeting, the following week. This time, the local fishermen were invited. J. Byers, W. Baxter and J.N. Armstrong attended. The chairman said "for a good time past, although a lot of fish has been landed at the port most of it is immediately sent away. We are in the peculiar position of having plenty of fish going past our doors and not a fish shop open in the town."

After some discussion, the meeting agreed on a number of points:-

1. A fish shop to be opened in Wampool St in charge of Mr Byers.

2. Committee to have the first call for local use on all fish caught.

3. No fish to be sold privately at the quay side.

4. Market price to be paid for all qualities of fish.

The chairman thanked the fisherman for the manner in which they had helped. Mr Byers duly opened the shop and, in 1928, his nephew, Joe Lomas, took it over.

One way round the meat shortage was to go out and shoot your own. There were always plenty of rabbits in the sandy banks along the coast.

'Tassy' Robinson of Wolsty seems to have been particularly successful in this area; perhaps it's how he made his living.

The members of the Holm Cultram Food Committee were:- Rev. R.A. Humble (Chairman), and Messrs A. Wilson, R. Holliday, J. Ostle, T.J. Armstrong, J. Roberts, C. Hawkins and W.D. Harvey. T.J. Haughan was the executive officer and V. Osborne was his assistant. An empty shop in Criffel Street was taken over for their office.

In September 1917, a member of the recently formed Silloth Labour Party wrote to the *Wigton Advertiser* expressing concern at the lack of working-class representation on the body. He didn't seem unduly worried that there were no women on it either!

RABBIT PIE

Skin the rabbit and cut it into joints. Melt 2ozs of butter in a pan, add the rabbit joints, 8ozs of bacon or ham, some onion and sprinkle well with salt and pepper. Add half-a-pint of vegetable stock and simmer gently for 45 minutes.

Leave until cold then fill a pie dish with the meat, cover with pastry and bake in a moderate oven for one-and-a-half hours. Brush the pastry over with milk when nearly done. (Serves 6)

Tassy Robinson. Run, Rabbit ....

late Captain Lattimer of the 'Kittiwake', and had been involved in a knitting party since the outbreak of war. During this time, she had produced 133 shirts, 103 pairs of socks, 30 handkerchiefs, 8 mufflers, 3 jerseys and 45 miscellaneous items – all hand worked and all for the soldiers at the front!

The good citizens of Aldoth did their bit for the troops at New Year, 1916. They beat Walt Disney by almost twenty years when they presented 'Snow White' in the school room there!

The heroinne was played by Miss Mabel Hethrington and Master Willie Morton (later a well-known Methodist preacher) was the prince.

Local farmer's lad, George Lightfoot, was one of the dwarfs. Miss Mary Sim accompanied the performers on the piano and the Rev. William Baxter took the chair. The front seats were 1/6d, Chairs were a shilling each but you could sit in a school desk for just ninepence!

Throughout the war years, many local women were involved in various forms of 'War Relief' work. In January 1917, The Holme St Cuthbert's group reported their collections for the previous year amounted to just over £77.

£29 had been spent on parcels sent to soldiers from the parish who were serving at the front. Many letters had been received from the troops expressing their "high appreciation" of these. Cigarettes and Tobacco were always the most popular items with the lads.

Donations had also been made to the Red Cross, The British Prisoners' Fund, The Blinded Soldiers' Fund and several other charities.

In October 1917, the *West Cumberland Times* congratulated 86-year-old Mrs Lattimer of Wampool Street, Silloth. She was the widow of the

Aldoth Mission Choir
An
Operetta
entitled
Snowwhite
and the Seven Dwarfs.
will be held in
Aldoth School Rooms
on
Thursday, Jan. 6th/16
&
Friday Jan. 7th/16
at 7 P.M.

To provide comforts for the Soldiers

A Dance will be held on Friday after the performance

CHAPTER THREE

LAST ORDERS

Some former pubs, now private homes.

The Oddfellows Arms, Blitterlees

The Foresters' Arms, Causewayhead.

The Ale House, Blooming Heather

The Anchor, Beckfoot

Over the twentieth century, many of the inns and ale houses which once dotted the Solway Plain have vanished. The process began in 1916 when Lloyd George introduced stringent controls on the sale of alcohol in the area under the 'State Management Scheme'.

In more recent times, other pubs have closed as part of a national trend and some large hotels have fallen victim to the ever-growing popularity of self-catering holidays.

This chapter recalls just a few of them.

The Carlisle and District State Management Scheme

During the First World War, a huge munitions factory was built near Gretna. By 1917, it was employing over 11,500 women and 5,000 men. The wages were high and the workers had little to spend them on apart from a visit to the pub. Drunkenness among the workers became a serious problem, especially in Carlisle.

The Lloyd George government took action. They bought two breweries in Carlisle and one in Maryport together with all the pubs they owned. The managers of the pubs received a weekly wage and thus had no incentive to sell large amounts of liquor. The scheme had a 'No Treating' policy – the buying of rounds was forbidden.

The government closed some pubs immediately and many others, over the next few years. The remainder offered alternatives to alcohol and some introduced food for the first time. After the war, rules were relaxed and the scheme built many new pubs designed by Harry Redfern, the scheme's own architect.

The SMS continued in operation until 1972 when the pubs were sold-off, mostly to the large brewery chains.

Allonby

Above: *Seven of Allonby's pubs.*

Below: *The pubs in the area behind the Ship Hotel.*

Nowhere has the closure process been quite as dramatic as in Allonby which, over the years, has had no less than ten pubs – serving a population of around 400!

The Spirit Vaults, located in the group of buildings which, in recent times, became the Riding School, was a traditional 'grog shop' selling rum directly from a huge barrel in the bar. It was run by the Costins who had family links with the West Indies and it is thought they imported the spirit directly from there.

The Ship was always Allonby's premier hostelry. Charles Dickens and Wilkie Collins stayed there in 1857. The Queen's Head was located at the other side of the bridge. It closed as a pub around 1850 and became a Temperance Hotel. The Grapes had opened by 1818 and was operated for many years by the Nichol family who also held other licences in the village.

The Solway Hotel opened around 1920. In 1962, the Bell family moved in and added a modern function room to the original house with its fifteen bedrooms. Friday 13th October 1973 was a really unlucky day for the Bells – the entire building was gutted by fire; it re-opened two years later. Then, during the 1980s, it had a new lease of life, re-named as the Ocean Liner. Business seems to have declined during the Nineties and finally, after yet another fire the building was demolished.

The Globe Inn, originally known as the London Apprentice, was located on the road to Westnewton and Aspatria. The village's three remaining hostelries were in the narrow lane behind The Ship. The Greyhound was located in Temple Square which was probably named after the family who owned the pub, while the Swan and the Sun both stood nearby.

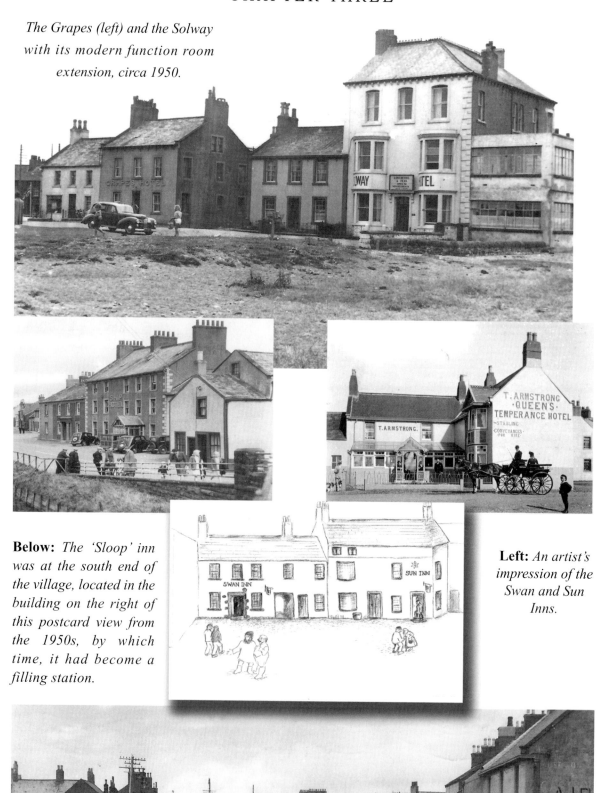

The Grapes (left) and the Solway with its modern function room extension, circa 1950.

Below: *The 'Sloop' inn was at the south end of the village, located in the building on the right of this postcard view from the 1950s, by which time, it had become a filling station.*

Left: *An artist's impression of the Swan and Sun Inns.*

Abbeytown

The old Wheatsheaf from the abbey roof. The Duke's Head is the building along the road with the triangular sign over the door.

In 1900 there were five pubs in Abbeytown: The Bush, The Wheatsheaf, The Masons' Arms, The Duke's Head and The Joiners' Arms. The Carlisle and District State Management Scheme took over in 1916 and, over the next few years, most of them closed.

In 1935, a brand new replacement opened. The new Wheatsheaf was designed by Harry Redfern, the scheme's own architect. It was a particularly fine example of his 'Country House' style. It included many features which supported the scheme's philosophy of reducing the intake of alcohol by providing both food and suitable facilities for ladies. The fine bowling green was seen as an alternative to spending too much time in the bar.

The Joiners' Arms – then and now.

The new Wheatsheaf, seen across its bowling green which has now become a car park,
Inset: *Harry Redfern's original plan for the ground floor of the pub.*

The Stingless Cup, Aikton

The Stingless Cup was a very unusual pub. It didn't sell Alcohol.

It was originally an ordinary village inn, called the Briscoe Arms. Then, in 1879, it was purchased by the local vicar, Cannon George Edmund Hassel, who turned it into a tee-total establishment.

Cannon Hassel was a member of the gentry; his family lived at Dalemain House on the shores of Ullswater. He set up a trust which let the house, rent free, to a couple on the understanding they would provide refreshments for villagers and travellers but would never serve alcohol. There was also a 'Reading Room' which, it was hoped, would attract the young men of the area and keep them away from the temptations of strong liquor.

Writing to *The Cumberland News* in 1951, Joe Bell of Morpeth recalled living in the pub around 1900. His uncle and aunt, Richard and Hannah Dalton were the tenants there. He remembered the summers when there were games of quoits and penny pitching as well as Cumberland and Westmorland Style Wrestling matches. His aunt baked gingerbread in six-inch squares which the farm lads bought for a penny together with a bottle of lemonade. Travellers could stable their horses and enjoy a meal of ham and eggs with bread and butter, followed by a slice of plate cake – all for sixpence!

Cannon Hassel left the village in 1910. The Stingless Cup stayed in business for a few more years but was eventually sold and became a private house.

Skinburness

Nobody really knows when the Longhouse at Skinburness was built. In the late 1700s, it was a pub called The Greyhound and the base for a ferry service to Annan. By the early 1900s, it had become a private hotel run by the Wannop family. It closed about 1933, the last manageress was a Mrs Orphan.

William and Margaret Wannop with staff and guests outside the hotel in 1912.

Judging from the comments in the visitors' book a good time was had by all.

Skinburness Hotel

Another tavern – The Dukes Head – originally stood on the site of the impressive Skinburness Hotel which opened in May 1887. It was built by E.H. Banks, a cotton manufacturer from Wigton who subsequently suffered severe financial problems and went bankrupt in 1908.

In 1916, the Carlisle State Management Scheme took it over and the hotel remained under their control until 1972. During these years, it was a pretty posh spot. It became the headquarters for many local clubs and societies and was a popular venue for weddings and other social gatherings.

After the break-up of the State Management Scheme, the Skinburness faced stiff new competition. The Solway Hotel, in Silloth town centre, had been taken-over by Ike Eilbeck, a successful local turkey farmer. He renamed it 'The Golf' and embarked on a thorough modernisation scheme. His efficient manager, Fausto Previtali, became a popular local personality and, slowly, the Skinburness lost much of its business to this new competitor.

The Skinburness passed through several different managements but never regained its previous popularity. It began to look decidedly shabby and old-fashioned in places. The last owners were Adrian and Vanessa Moore, a couple from the North-East. They concentrated on the coach party trade and re-opened the ballroom. However, the venture was unsuccessful and the Moores, like E.H. Banks before them, were declared bankrupt. Their total debts amounted to more than £1.2 million. The hotel finally closed its doors in September 2006.

The Hotel in the early 1900s.

The Original Interior.

Left: *A view in the 1950s.*

The Board Inn, Pelutho (say it 'Pellata').

Stewarton House, formerly the Board Inn.

Hugh Hutton purchased The Board Inn, Pelutho in 1904 for £1,200. It was a 'free house' and, judging from reports in the local press, a bit of a rough house too.

When his licence came up for renewal in February 1905, the police objected. They claimed that Hutton had been breaching the Sunday licensing regulations and that the business was "carried on largely for the purpose of dancing and attracting young people to the place."

Hutton admitted to hiring out a barn to a man named Johnston to hold a dance there and said it had, probably been a foolish thing to do but "there was no great crime in it." The police spokesman claimed "the licensee was the moving spirit in the dance. He cleared the place out, gave them lemonade boxes and forms to sit upon, and let the ladies go to a room to change their dresses, (laughter in court)." It was also suggested that gambling had been taking place in the pub.

After giving the magistrates an undertaking to mend his ways, Hutton's license was renewed but, by September, there was more trouble.

William Brough, a farmer from Hards, who weighed between sixteen and eighteen stones, arrived at the pub, already drunk. Hutton refused to serve him and, with help from another customer, Peter Carruthers of Cobble Hall, threw him out onto the road where he turned on both the men.

Later in court, Mrs Hutton said she thought Brough was killing Carruthers, he "had him by the back of the neck and was banging him on the seat. He was like a madman – a fanatic".

Asked if Carruthers was a regular customer at the pub, Mrs Hutton said "No, I call a man a regular when he calls every day." Brough was fined £1.

In 1909, the police again opposed renewal of the licence. A commercial traveller, Mr J.H. Hampson of Wigton, told the court he had used the house for seven years and slept there four times a year, always being made very comfortable. Despite this glowing testimonial, the bench refused to renew Hutton's licence and, later, awarded him £600 in compensation for its loss .

At the hearing, the pub's accounts were inspected. During the year it had got through 48 barrels of beer, 162 dozen bottles of beer, 302 gallons of spirits and 17 gallons of cordials and wine. The Locals must have missed the place.

Cheers, Dennis!

Many, many thanks to Dennis Irwin of Carlisle for his help with this chapter. Look out for Dennis's forthcoming book on the pubs and alehouses of Cumbria.

CHAPTER FOUR

1919 – 1938, The Twenties and Thirties

Silloth Sea Front in the 1920s

This was a period of great social change, economic decline, political instability and industrial unrest. Britain was never the same after 1918 and its domination of world affairs took a major blow from which it never recovered.

Heavy industries and mining declined. Many workers were laid off and there were dramatic consequences in neighbouring areas. There were prolonged strikes in the coal mines at Aspatria and West Cumberland was badly hit by the depression. By 1933, almost sixty per cent of Maryport's workforce was unemployed.

The Solway Plain was barely affected by all this but, nevertheless, a number of changes happened during these years.

There was a great increase in motor traffic, reducing the role of rail in the transport of people and goods. There was an influx of ordinary working families by rail and bus for holidays at Silloth and Allonby while the wealthier ones, who had come to the area in great numbers, now went abroad or to southern England.

Two major organisational changes took place. Firstly, the railways were formed into four large, national companies. The Carlisle to Silloth line now became part of the LNER network. This large company inherited much of Silloth including the port.

Despite the tiny role of Silloth within the LNER Empire, one advantage was that the resort could be advertised in a much wider spread of locations. This was the era of the railway art posters, which were seen at stations all over the UK. Silloth was being brought to the attention of far more people than ever before.

The second change was the restructuring of local government. 1934 saw the Holm Cultram, Wigton and Aspatria districts amalgamated into a single 'Wigton Rural District' council. This caused much dismay among ratepayers and council members. Money was now being put in a pot to be spread over a large area and the new council would not be devoted to Holm Cultram as before. However, a town council was formed for Silloth.

The 1919 housing act gave local councils the power to provide homes for people, and some were built on the plain to ease overcrowding. The lower rents helped poorer families.

Hotels struggled but boarding houses were well used, and a new form of holiday emerged – the home made, self-catering retreat. People began to put huts, caravans and old road and rail vehicles along the shore to use as holiday homes – something which was not welcomed by the sanitation - conscious local council!

Local industry fared pretty well, both the flour mill and chemical works at Silloth remained busy.

New services appeared; Radio transmission began and 'wireless' receivers were available in local shops. By 1934, mains electricity had come to Abbeytown and Silloth but life on the farms and in the country went on virtually unchanged.

Two of the fine posters promoting Silloth,   issued by the LNER.

Skinburness and the old creek bridge.

The Trippers

West beach in the 1930s. The pier is showing the first signs of subsidence.

In 1923, Silloth's rail link became part of the LNER network. Soon after the take-over, the company introduced cheap day-return tickets from Carlisle. These proved to be immensely popular with ordinary working families from the city.

For the next thirty years, hoards of day-trippers descended on Silloth every fine weekend in the summer. On Bank Holidays, the numbers arriving were truly amazing. During the Whit Weekend in 1933, 7,000 people travelled to the town by train. In 1937, the Holiday Weekend in August was especially hot. The *Carlisle Journal* reported

Crowds of day-trippers on the green. On the left, Thomas Gass, who was previously in business as a blacksmith, advertises his newly-opened motor works. A group of unemployed men seem to be hanging about on the corner.

54

that it was "hard to find a place to sit on the seafront at Silloth". 1,100 rail tickets had been sold on Saturday, and 5,000 the following Monday.

Most of the trippers got off the train, took the footpath past the golf club and headed for West Beach. Here, they could buy refreshments and enjoy the other simple pleasures of the seaside. It must have been a wonderful escape for the people of Carlisle which, at that time, was a grimy, smoky, industrial city with a great deal of poor housing.

Some stayed overnight in tents. However, the lack of public toilets meant that the Convalescent Home was constantly approached by people wishing to use theirs – a situation deplored by the management!

Other visitors headed for the town centre and the green. Here, the Victorian baths had closed and been converted into a tea room but a new putting green had opened. Mr Gray offered donkey rides on the green. Mrs Baxter's new tearooms overlooked the shore and, with several cafes and more than one fish and chip shop, there was plenty of choice at lunch or tea times.

There were often Brass Band concerts and other entertainments. Deck chairs were available for hire and many older people just spent the day admiring the view across the Solway.

Some visitors were more adventurous and took a boat trip. Most of the local fishermen supplemented their income in the summer months by offering these trips. Some boats just sailed around for half-an-hour or so while others offered a full excursion over the water to Annan on the Scottish side.

The Putting Green, opened in the 1920s.

The Phillips family

were one of many Carlisle families who headed for Silloth at holiday time. They are grouped here on the west beach in the 1930s. The convalescent home can be seen behind the dunes on the right. Jack Phillips (top left) was a warehouse foreman at Carrs' biscuit works.

Giving pleasure to many children at Silloth during these years were the donkey rides. Chris 'Donkey' Gray, looked after them for Sarah Gray.

Some of Sidney Martin's atmospheric shots of the sailing boats...

Maritime Matters

Large steamer Michael E Tricoglu arrives in June 1929 with Tunisian phosphate.

The docks at Silloth had been badly affected by the 1914-18 war. The daily service to Liverpool was no longer viable and the ships were sold. Foreign trade all but ceased. Economically the next two decades were unsettled and difficult, but trade improved and, by the 1930s, wood was being imported again from Russia and Nova Scotia. A stream of coasters brought grain to Carrs' flour Mill and slates still came in from Wales. Mineral ores came in from a variety of places for Maxwell's Fertilizer works and coal exports continued to Ireland.

A new trade was the export of coke to Norway. This came from the gas works at Carlisle and was a by-product of coal. Tin plate was brought from South Wales for Hudson Scott, the metal box makers in Carlisle.

The Yarrow's scheduled runs to Dublin continued but, in 1929, the ship was renamed 'Assaroe' and registered in Dublin. She continued to call at the Isle of Man during the summer, taking many people to memorable holidays on the Island. The port continued to interest and entertain people as ships, large and small, steamed in and out.

The Solway Lightship

In 1922, a new tourist attraction appeared, probably the most original and unusual one of all. For many years a light vessel had been anchored off Allonby to guide shipping into the Solway. It was manned by crews who lived on board for days on a rota basis. The lightship, on a number of occasions, found herself ashore after stormy seas broke the anchoring, sending her off to various parts of the Solway.

In 1920 the ageing boat was decommissioned and, for a while lay in the dock at Silloth, but her career was not over yet. Someone saw potential in this long serving and familiar hulk. Local plumber and gas fitter, William Ferguson (Father of entertainer A. C. Astor), purchased the boat and had it towed up the coast by tug on a high tide so it could be left on the beach. After cleaning it up, he gave it a new use – as a teashop and visitor attraction. With a set of steps up to the main deck, tourists walking to and from Skinburness could now call in, explore the old ship and buy refreshments. The vessel was put up for sale in 1926 but no buyer was found and she was eventually dismantled for the salvage value of her timbers and metalwork.

The lightship beached off Skinburness Road.

A number of men were still employed at the port. Among them were.....

Joe Baxter – Dockgateman
Tom Johnston - Labourer
Bill Archer – Dockgateman
John Sim - Craneman
Gus Proud – Stevedore
Joe Nelson – Coal trimmer
Luke Woodhouse – Labourer
Frank Woodhouse – Bargeman
John Minnican – Labourer
Norman Reed – Labourer
Robert Cartner – Dock porter
John Slack - Labourer

*The 'Gertie' arriving with wheat from
Liverpool*

A busy scene at the docks in July 1930. The long vessel whose bow is on the far right had brought phosphate from Tampa, Florida. A coaster delivers wheat to the mill.
The hydraulic coal hoist can be seen in the centre of the photograph. A railway wagon full of coal is waiting at the foot of the machine. It would be lifted to the top of the gantry and then tipped on its end, allowing the coal to run down the chute into the ship's hold.

You can see a movie of the hoist in action on the website: www.solwayplain.co.uk/silloth2.htm

1927: Coasters with wheat for the mill lie astern of the Uddeholm loaded with Swedish wood.

Welsh slates are stacked in the foreground.

Stan Graham remembers . . .

In 1938, when I was 18, I went for my first holiday without the family. I took the 'Asseroe' from Silloth to the Isle of Man and stayed at Cunningham's Holiday Camp, just outside Douglas.

The accommodation was in chalets, it was quite cosy.

The Assaroe leaves Silloth, late 1930s

There were three of us in together – the other lads were strangers to me. I'd met a lad I knew on Carlisle station and so I 'palled-up' with him for the week I was there.

There were good sports facilities on the camp – I remember playing football and bowls. In the evenings we used to go into Douglas to the Villa Marina and various other places.

Cunnigham's Young Men's Holiday camp was established by Joseph Cunningham in 1894 when the accommodation was in tents. The chalets were built during World War I to house enemy aliens.

I don't recall much about the 'Asseroe' – it was just a boat! The crossing was a bit rough, it took five-and-a-half hours to get to Douglas and I felt very sick. It was better coming home; they had picked-up a lot of cattle in Dublin and their weight seemed to keep the ship on a more even keel.

A bird's eye view

In 1929 a plane flew over Silloth and one of the occupants took a series of photographs which were reproduced on postcards and were the first aerial views of the town.

In 1923 William English set up Silloth Products, a company which made confectionary. Mr English was a local man, originally a labourer on the railway, who then set up as a coal agent and carter. Feeling that a resort like Silloth would benefit from its own unique range of foods, he applied to build premises where he could manufacture these and a factory was built on Esk Street.

Here, a small workforce, using their own recipes, made various wares including 'Silloth Toffee' and a patent 'Wholegrain health meal'. The business was sadly a short-lived one, lasting only 5 years. Perhaps someone still has the recipes?

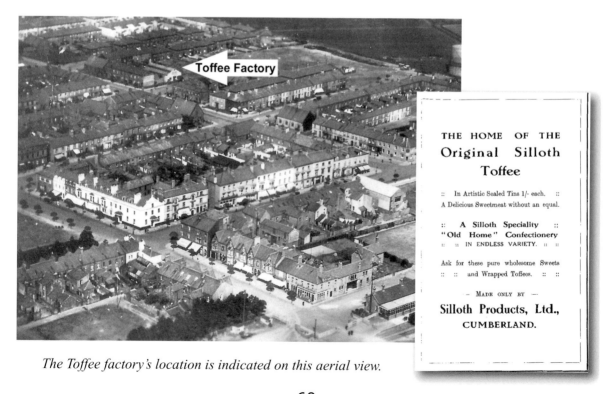

THE HOME OF THE
Original Silloth Toffee

:: In Artistic Sealed Tins 1/- each. ::
A Delicious Sweetmeat without an equal.

:: A Silloth Speciality ::
"Old Home" Confectionery
:: :: IN ENDLESS VARIETY. :: ::

Ask for these pure wholesome Sweets
:: :: and Wrapped Toffees. :: ::

— MADE ONLY BY —
Silloth Products, Ltd.,
CUMBERLAND.

The Toffee factory's location is indicated on this aerial view.

Town and Country Life

Being a fairly new, planned town, Silloth's houses were well built and relatively spacious. Rows of small homes also existed at places like Raglan Court, but they were far from poor. By the standards of the day, Silloth was one of the best quality urban areas anywhere.

By the 1930s, the District Council was actively improving the housing, renovating some and demolishing others which were 'unfit for habitation'. They also began building new houses. The 1919 housing act gave them the power to erect and let homes at low rents for less well-off families. This was possible due to funds from central government subsidising the cost.

By 1925, an estate of council homes had been built at Silloth, a row at Abbeytown and a pair at Beckfoot. In the villages, however, many of the homes were small and dated from before the nineteenth century.

Allonby

Allonby, from the seafront, presented a line of well-built Georgian villas – but behind this facade were many lanes and courts with small, closely clustered dwellings, dating back to the eighteenth century.

The village remained popular with visitors. Several hotels and boarding houses catered for them, along with a new phenomenon – the camping fields. Allonby grew popular with motorists, and holidays meant cars parked all over the open spaces near the village.

Caldew Street was typical of Silloth homes. Note the open skylights in the roof. All the attics were bedrooms too. Beyond, in this 1920s view, the new council houses are under construction around Latrigg Street.

The girls are passing Bessie Stalker's shop, later Berry's.

The 1921 Council Houses at Beckfoot were also among the first to be built in the area.

Pat Antolak remembers . . .

In the late 1930s, Pat's father was the vicar of Allonby. She recalls some village customs:-

"Allonby itself was a strange little place, there was the chapel, the Friends' meeting house and the Church of England. The church was really on the outskirts of the parish. Because, when it was built, the Quakers weren't welcoming the Church; the village was very wrapped-up with the Friends. So the church was built outside the toll bar which was about a hundred yards away. It was the dividing line."

"When there were marriages, it was the custom for the children to put a rope across the road from the toll bar to the house on the other side. You had to pay to get through and be married."

"At the time of a funeral, there was a wonderful little hearse with glass sides. It was hand-drawn by three men – no horses or anything like that. And the custom was to have what they called a 'Bidder'. It was nothing to do with an auctioneer. The Bidder was a chosen lady of the village who had to dress herself all in black. She would never speak but would present herself at your door if you were invited to the funeral tea. She used to present you with a card which was an invitation to the tea – that was the bidding for you to come to the party. You had to reply, of course."

Allonby Vicarage.

The Sunshine Home

Allonby's Sunshine Home, originally known as the Robinson Harrison Fresh Air Home, opened in August 1933. It was founded by Mrs Margaret Harriet Ann Harrison of Scalesceugh Hall, near Carlisle in memory of her husband – Robinson Harrison. It provided a week's holiday for under-privileged children from Carlisle and West Cumberland.

Although the day-to-day running of the home was in the hands of a local committee, the Harrison family retained ownership of the land and building for many years.

Mawbray W.I. Stall

In the late 1930s, the Mawbray Women's Institute ran a cake and produce stall. Ada Nattrass was in charge on the day this picture was taken and that's a young John Nattrass lying on the ground to the left.

The stall was strategically situated on the coast road to pick-up the passing trade from motorists and ramblers. It was on the triangle of grass at the turn-off to the village. The building in the background is the County Council Shed which was built on the site of the original village school.

Abbeytown
John Hurst remembers the 1930s

I was born there in 1928, the eldest son of John and Mary Jane Hurst. Father was the local 'man from the Pru' and my maternal Grandmother, Mary Little, ran the village shop together with Aunt Florry.

We lived at a house called Oakville, next to the Beckton family. Mrs Beckton used to give me many gifts of grapes from their vinery.

When about five, my father's work took us away from the village but both of my Grandmothers remained and I returned to spend holidays with them.

Abbeytown, or t'Abba as it was called by locals, had shops, a post office, a pub (The Wheatsheaf), church, chapel and school, as well as a garage, run by the Mattinson Brothers. Joe Huddart made daily deliveries of milk in his horse and trap and Nick Henderson conveyed fruit and veg by pony and flat cart.

Grandma Little's was a talking shop where customers chatted while purchasing. A confectioner, called Bessie, baked bread and cakes on the premises and one of my strongest memories is of the flavour of newly baked bread with a slab of butter melting on it. The cold meats counter in there was also a favourite place from which I was allowed to take occasional samples.

Grandma Little, as well as running the shop, kept pigs and hens and, every Saturday morning, she caught the bus to Carlisle to sell her eggs in market there.

Nick Henderson, fruit and veg merchant.

A Hired Lass

Young Fanny Lightfoot came from Wigton. At Whitsuntide 1923, she was hired as a domestic servant by James Hutton and his wife who farmed at The Wath, near Silloth. For twenty-six weeks' work she was to be paid £22 plus board and lodging. She stuck at the job for eleven weeks but didn't really get on with her new master and mistress. She did her best but they were continually grumbling about her work.

One Sunday morning, in late August, things came to a head. Fanny got up at 5.30am. She laid and lit two coal fires. Then she had to rouse the farm lads from their beds and clean the kitchen range before going outside to hand milk eight cows. After this, she went back to the farmhouse, made the lads their breakfast, washed the milk tins and scrubbed the kitchen floor.

At 9.15, her mistress finally came downstairs and accused Fanny of not having cleaned the grate. This was the last straw. Fanny said she thought it would be best if she looked for a new job and allowed the Huttons to "get somebody else to do the work to please you." Mrs Hutton said "Very well, you can go!"

Mr Hutton didn't get up until twelve o'clock. Fanny asked him for her wages to date totalling £11. "No, not today – it's Sunday", he replied. The girl stayed at the farm overnight but, on Monday morning, Hutton still refused to pay her. She left and asked for her belongings to be sent on to her on the milk cart.

By October, Fanny still hadn't received her wages or her trunk and everybody ended up in court at Silloth where she sued the Huttons for her dues. They insisted that nothing had happened to cause Fanny to leave her job and that the position was still open if she wanted to come back.

Judge Gawan Taylor said he thought the events of the Sunday morning showed that Fanny was a capable girl and he was sure she was truthful. He awarded the full £11 owing to her.

The Wath, A picture postcard view produced by Martins of Silloth in the 1920s.

Motoring

The 1920s and 30s witnessed a steady rise in motor traffic. Although cars were beyond most people's income, the Solway coast became a popular destination for motorists from outside the area seeking a day trip. By 1937, the *Carlisle Journal* was reporting that on a Sunday "the banks between Allonby and Silloth resembled one vast car park"

The first regular motor bus services began in 1921, connecting Maryport, Allonby and Silloth, and Silloth with Carlisle. These, along with vans belonging to commercial travellers, became a frequent sight.

To support those visitors and residents with cars, a handful of the people set up new businesses. These provided fuel, undertook repairs, charged batteries and sold accessories. They also provided cars for hire and taxi services, in addition to other mechanical engineering work.

By the 1930s, Silloth had three motor engineers – Thomas Gass at Seaview, Robert Stobie at the Hydro garage on Waver Street and the Silloth Motor & Engineering Company on Petteril Street. At Abbeytown, the Mattinson Brothers ran a filling station and repair shop and, at Allonby, there was the Central Garage, run by Robert Clark and, later, by James Twentyman. Sidney Thompson also ran a service station.

All over the area, the people enthusiastically embraced the internal combustion engine!

Eden Street, Silloth, just after the first world war.

Early bus on Eden Street, Silloth.

Even in Mawbray, the internal combustion engine had arrived!

The spacious, purpose-built premises of Silloth Motor & Engineering Co.
This photo was taken soon after it was established in 1929.

Allonby Green and the Central Garage.

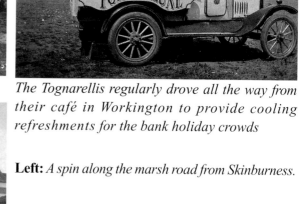
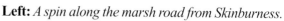

The Tognarellis regularly drove all the way from their café in Workington to provide cooling refreshments for the bank holiday crowds

Left: *A spin along the marsh road from Skinburness.*

Below: *August Bank Holiday crowds at Allonby in 1937. The picture shows their methods of transport: cars, bikes and motorcycles. Some would have come on the bus from Maryport.*

Farming

Farming on the Solway Plain had hardly changed since the turn of the century. There was little mechanisation and only a few farms had electricity. The average holding was between 60 and 100 acres.

A report, published in 1936, takes a larger farm at Allonby as an example of typical practice in the inter-war years. A total of 200 acres were divided as follows:-

       23 acres of potatoes

       31 acres of wheat

       23 acres of barley

       8 acres of oats

       8 acres of turnips

       107 acres of pasture

Harry Glencross at Smarthill Farm, Aldoth in the 1930s.
Heavy Horses were still the main motive power on all farms at this time.

Barley was a fairly unusual crop in the area. This farmer sold his crop as malting grain to make beer. The turnips were grown primarily for animal food. In the autumn, farmers would travel to the sheep auctions in Scotland to buy fattened lambs. These were kept in the fields, feeding off the root crops, until Christmas when they were sent to market locally.

Local people were predominately dairy farmers. The Shorthorn was the most popular breed of cattle and was sometimes cross-bred with the Ayrshire. The milk was collected from the farms by lorry and taken to the Milk Marketing Board depot at Aspatria.

A few farms had begun to specialise in poultry. Only one, near Abbeytown, relied entirely on selling eggs. Some sold fertilised eggs or day-old chicks. Others sold oven-ready birds. Chicken was still a luxury food at this time and the local market was pretty limited.

The authors of the 1936 report noted "there is an almost entire absence of any market garden developments on what would be very suitable land in a district very accessible to an important centre like Carlisle. There have been remarkably few developments of holiday facilities and there appear to be still fewer developments in local farming and gardening to cater for the holiday-makers who visit the coast."

They concluded "Farming has remained on stereotyped lines and the methods in this district have probably altered as little during recent years as in any other district in the North."

Threshing Day at Cowgate, Mawbray about 1925.

John Ostle, the farmer stands, with his handcart, in the centre of a group of family and friends who have come to help. The threshing machine and the traction engine which provided the power would be hired from a contactor for a few days. The farmer was responsible for supplying the coal.

The Cumberland Pig

During the first half of the twentieth century, the Cumberland Pig was immensely popular with local farmers. Its floppy ears, flat face and smooth silky coat distinguished it from other, lesser breeds. It was a source of the legendary Cumberland Ham and provided the distinctive flavour to Cumberland Sausage.

Almost all the farms on the Solway Plain would keep at least one pig. Slaughtered at the 'back-end' of the year, it would provide the farmer's own family with a supply of good tasty ham and bacon through the winter. There might even be enough left to send a few sides of bacon to Maryport market!

Eamont Peter Pan

First Prize Winner at Royal Lancashire Show and awarded The Silver Challenge Cup for Best Cumberland Pig, 1927.

The county's biggest pig farms were around Carlisle, Penrith and along the Eden Valley but Kirkbride was also an important area for pig farming. Thomas Wills of Angerton House there was a well-known breeder.

In 1915, he attended a meeting of farmers in the King's Arms Inn at Wigton. The meeting was convened by Mr T. B. Schofield, the government's local livestock officer and Mr Steel, the Wigton vet. Mr Schofield told the meeting that his department were spending hundreds of pounds each year buying boars. These were then made available to small farmers for breeding purposes. However, the Cumberland Pig did not qualify for the scheme although the farmers were anxious to use it. The problem was that there was no 'Pedigree System' and so the breed was not officially recognised.

The meeting resolved to form a Cumberland Pig Breeders Association and to establish a 'Herd Book' which would register all pure-bred Cumberlands and so make them eligible for the government's breeding programme.

Gate Mary

Second Prize Winner at Yorkshire Agricultural Show.

The farmers present at the meeting pledged £75 to get things going and appointed a council to oversee operations. Over the next few years, more than one hundred farms signed up for the Herd Book. These included a good number of those situated on the Solway Plain.

Tom Wills served as a council member for the new association along with his neighbour Joseph Robinson of Wampool Farm. J. Carr of Whitrigg House, The Graham brothers of Whitriglees and Greenspot, and J. Mark of Angerton were also registered breeders. The Lowthers, Liddles, Nichols and Robinsons were other families from Kirkbride who appeared regularly in the Herd Book.

A sad end to the story . . .

In 1955, the government's Advisory Committee on Pig Production produced a report which indicated that housewives were then demanding a leaner type of meat. They recommended that farmers should concentrate on only three breeds: the Large White, the Welsh and the Landrace. The breeding stock of the Cumberland began to decline and, even before the report was published, there were only three breeding boars registered in the county.

The last individual, a sow belonging to a Mr Thirwell of Bothel Craggs died in 1960 and the breed became extinct.

Janet II
Second Prize Winner at Royal Lancashire Show.

John Routledge of Old Silloth Farm was a very successful breeder of Cumberland Pigs. In 1921, he showed a boar which won the Breeders' Association Show at Penrith and was then sold for 90 guineas. In 1923, he sold a champion sow for 81 guineas. His best breeding sow was 'Seabreeze

of Old Silloth' whose litter of eleven six-month old piglets was sold for 320 guineas. John was vice-chairman of the Holm Cultram Agricultural Society.

He died in January 1924 when he choked, ironically on a piece of pork, while dining with friends at the Criffel Hotel. His widow, Margaret, continued to breed the pigs for many more years.

SOME OTHER LOCAL FARMERS WHO BRED CUMBERLAND PIGS.

T J Armstrong of Doucie Farm, Calvo.
P R Foster of Allonby
Thomas Hodgson of Mawbray Farm
J Hornsby of Holme Lea, Silloth
W Penrice of Park House, Silloth
John Slack, Holme Low, Silloth

Silloth Show

Presenting the awards

The Holm Cultram Agricultural Society organised this annual event in a field off Skinburness Road. It gave the farming community a rare day-off and a chance to exchange news and gossip.

The farmers paraded their best livestock. The classes for Shorthorn Cattle and Clydesdale Horses attracted entries from all over the county. There were exhibitions of saddle and harness horses, a dog show and show-jumping.

The farmers' wives also had a chance to show off their skills. There were competitions for baking, knitting, quilting, poker work, and jam and chutney making.

Both farm servants and local gardeners could enter the produce contests. There were sections for Swedes, Carrots, Mangold Wurtzels and Common Turnips among many others.

The latest technology in use.

Out on the marsh

The marshlands around Skinburness and Calvo have always provided excellent grazing for sheep and cattle.

In the 20s and 30s, each farmer in the district was entitled to keep some of his stock there. He would be allocated a number of 'stints' on the marsh. One stint entitled him to graze one head of cattle or one ewe and her lambs. The number of stints depended on the size of his farm. For holdings between 70 and 100 acres, the number of stints could vary from four to eleven. If he didn't want to use his full allocation, he could let his stints to a neighbour.

In winter, when the marsh is often subject to tidal flooding, the stock would be brought back to the farm. The Marsh Committee then let the grazing rights to farmers from the Lake District who kept sheep there.

In November 1920, 1,300 sheep arrived to spend their winter on the marsh. These Herdwicks had been driven, on foot, from the fells around Buttermere. They were mostly 'Gimmer Hogs' – the farmers' valuable breeding stock for the next year. The Marsh Committee appointed Thomas Jefferson of Calvo as their shepherd.

He was expected to keep his eye on the sheep and to move the flock if flooding threatened them. He was paid nine pence per head for this work which extended from November until 25th March. Due to bad weather, the sheep could not be moved until March 29th when Jefferson took them to Abbeytown where they were reclaimed by their owners.

He received no payment for these four extra days' work and, the following October, sued the Marsh Committee for unpaid wages. His was the first case to be heard at the newly opened Silloth County Court.

During the proceedings, it transpired that, over the winter, 272 sheep had been lost due to flooding. Jefferson admitted to loosing 32 but, in his defence said that, in some previous years, as many as 600 head had been lost.

The judge said he thought that the shepherd's job must have been very difficult with 1,200 acres to watch. However, there were no dates specified in the contract and he found in favour of the Marsh Committee.

There are accounts of sheep being lost to high tides elsewhere on the coast. In 1926, Jerry Richardson, a hill farmer from Gatesgarth, lost 57 out of 60 'hogs' to a high tide at Rockcliffe. Despite these losses, the practice of wintering Herdwicks on the marshes seems to have continued until the war years.

Fashion Page

In the 1920s, women liberated themselves from the constricting fashions of Edwardian times. They began to wear more comfortable clothes such as short skirts and slacks with separate blouses or jumpers. Men also abandoned overly formal clothes in favour of sports jackets and trousers. New fabrics, such as Rayon came into use. Hair styles changed dramatically; the 'Bob' and the Marcel Wave were particularly popular. The tight fitting Cloche hat became an icon of fashion.

Above: *This group of friends are taking the sun beside Allonby Reading Room in the very early 20s. They demonstrate the new trends very well. The young ladies are wearing skirts and blouses; the girl sitting on the wall has a V-neck top. The older ladies dress more conservatively but are showing their ankles! The young man is in 'Plus Fours'.*

Above: *The wedding of Richard Ostle and Mary Stanwix in April, 1921 was a pretty smart affair. Mary's veil is similar to that worn by Lady Elizabeth Bowes-Lyon at her marriage to the future King George VI.*

Left: *Norah Edgar sports the newest in hair-dos.*

Above: *Schoolteacher, Catherine Osborne (left) and her friend show off the latest styles.*

Above: *By the 1930s, skirts had got shorter and the cloche hat had become popular. Things were far less formal. The models are from Abbeytown Tennis Club.*

A local flapper.

Cissie Beake

Cissie's full name was Christiana, she was a music teacher and lived on Burnswark Terrace in Silloth from 1925 until sometime around 1940. She was great friends with the Arnison sisters who ran the confectionery business across the road. Her family originated from Yorkshire but her father was a railway engine driver who moved to Carlisle in 1910.

She was a staunch Wesleyan and was fondly remembered by many of the older members of the chapel. They say she always wore long, black clothes. Cathy Cornish (née Carr) took piano lessons with Cissie. This stood her in good stead when she used to play for her brother, Billy, and his friends in the Pierotts.

Shirley Sim was another pupil. She thought Cissie's methods were a bit old-fashioned and she didn't like the way the canary was allowed to fly around the music room.

After her brother's death, in 1938, Cissie moved away and helped look after his children.

CHAPTER FIVE

An Industrial Interlude

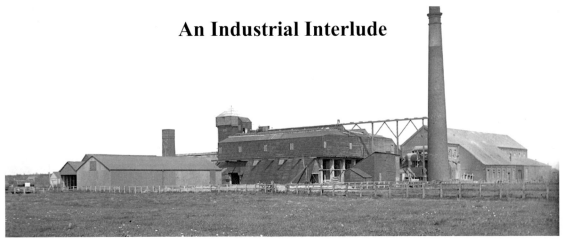

J & W Maxwell's Solway Chemical Works around 1900

Silloth Chemical Works

William Crabb, who came from Kirriemuir in north-east Scotland, established the first chemical works at Silloth in 1870. Over the next two decades it prospered and increased its capacity, employing a number of local men. Some of them lived in a specially built row of four homes nearby, known originally as Crabb's cottages and later as Chemical Cottages.

In 1877, a second factory was built. A partnership of three Carlisle merchants, James Graham, William Maxwell, and John Fairlie initially set up the business to manufacture phosphate and other fertilizers. Five years later, the business was restyled in the name of J & W Maxwell & Sons.

Both factories used a variety of raw materials. Most arrived by sea. Phosphate rock came from the United States and, later, from North Africa. Guano (bird droppings) came from South America. Mineral ore and Pyrites came from Spain while Kainit and Potash were imported from Germany. Inside the works, Sulphur Ore was burned and the fumes used to make sulphuric acid. This was mixed into the phosphate rock, which had been ground-up by heavy rollers, and the result was 'Superphosphate'.

This was the primary product, but various grades and types of fertilizer were created by adding other minerals such as potash. The sulphuric acid was also used to dissolve animal bones and create bone meal manure.

The main processes were burning, grinding and blending. The various blends were conveyed to a large warehouse area where they were packed in hessian sacks made on site. These were then put directly onto rail wagons – both factories had sidings into their warehouses – and sent for distribution. Some was delivered locally by horse and cart or, later, by lorries.

In 1899 Maxwells acquired Crabb's Border Counties works and the latter then ceased operations. The buildings were later dismantled and the site was cleared in the 1930s.

Maxwells prospered and their factory expanded. Many local people worked at the site, which was known locally as 'The Chemics'. The plant had over 100 staff during the busy spring and autumn seasons. The products were sold under the brand 'Maxman-ure'.

John Maxwell died in 1928, and his brother, William, in 1943. With no successors, the

Danish Steamer 'Sigurd' arriving with phosphate from Sfax, Tunisia for J & W Maxwell in June 1914

"Success is sure with Maxmanure"

family firm's works were sold to Langdales & Northern Fertilizers in 1940 and they became part of the Fisons empire shortly afterwards.

At first, Fisons invested in modernising the plant, adding a new warehouse and production areas but, by the 1960s, a national rationalisation policy was adopted. Cheaper, ready-made fertilizers were being imported from the continent and threatened the entire British manure trade. Fisons choose to invest in a large modern plant at Immingham. Their small plants were closed down and Silloth made its last fertilizer in 1962. The employees were offered work at other sites. A handful of workers were kept on as it was decided to use Silloth to store and distribute products made elsewhere.

The production areas, some dating from the 1880s, were demolished, leaving only the newer warehouses. After 10 years the depot closed and the site, known as the Harvest Industrial estate, was bought by local entrepreneur, Philip Harker.

The Managers

During its life, the factory had three managers. The first and longest serving was Henry Lindsay Barker. He came to Silloth from Perth where he had studied chemical engineering. He was a popular character who disliked authority. In later years, when not at work he enjoyed riding his motorcycle. His daughter, Mabel, became a keen walker and climber, scaling many of the challenging rock climbs in the Lake District and beyond – something unheard of for a woman at that time. She was a pioneer of education too, advocating outdoor experience for young people and taking groups into the fells.

Henry eventually retired, at the age of seventy-five, in 1930. His replacement was Arthur Wilson. During his time, the fifty-year old plant was rebuilt and updated. Arthur played a key role in this. In 1934, he designed and patented a new device known as the Maxwell 'Den'. This was a large structure with a revolving container which enabled automatic continuous production of Superphosphate.

Arthur Wilson retired in the late 1950s. The last manager of the works was Eric Laws who had begun work there in 1933, working his way up from the shop floor.

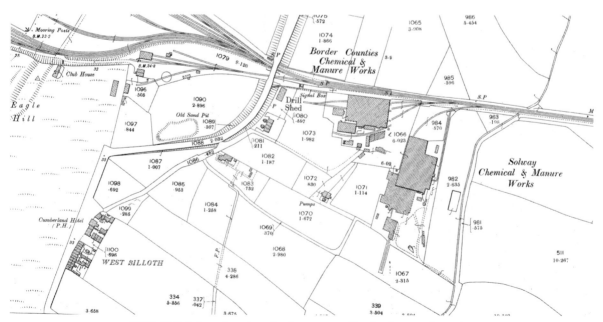

1901 O.S. Map showing the location of both chemical works.

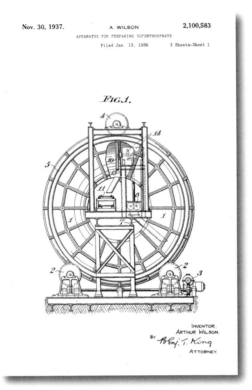

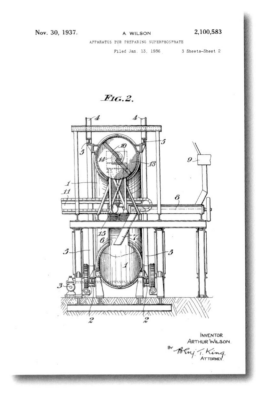

Arthur Wilson's device for the production of Superphosphate and diagrams from his patent grant.

Eric Laws remembers life at the plant...

When I first went there, it was J & W Maxwells. They had a base in Carlisle – Kings Arms lane. There was quite a big store in there. The lane wasn't wide and we had to back lorries into it! Maxwells used to sell farm seeds as well, The farm seeds were all mixed and bagged at Kings Arms Lane.

The late Eric Laws with his wife, Eva.

The Maxwells lived on Norfolk Road in Carlisle.

Well, Maxwells were taken over by Langdales & Northern Fertilizers. They had a fertilizer works at St Peters in Newcastle, and another at Blaydon. About a year later, Fisons came in and they took the lot over.

Raw materials

We used to get phosphate from Christmas Island, and another Island called Nauru. That was a very high grade phosphate. We also got a lot from Morocco; it had sharks teeth in it. It came from Russia too, that was a fine type that didn't need grinding. It was volcanic phosphate. The other thing we used to import a lot of was Pyrites it came from Huelva. I remember one shipment of Pyrites we got in; I think it was about 3,700 tons. At the time it was the biggest cargo ever brought into Silloth dock. The ship was anchored off Allonby for about a fortnight, waiting for high enough water.*

Potash we mostly got from Israel. There was a little bit came from a place in Cheshire too. Sulphate of ammonia we took from Carlisle Gas works and from

*Eric is referring to a ship called the SONJA, which brought over 3,000 tonnes of copper ore from Huelva, Spain in November 1937

ICI; Trainloads of it came in from their works at Billingham on the East coast.

Producing the fertilizer

We had the furnace house, with two blocks of fires with six on each side. They were charged every hour. The Pyrites or Sulphur ore was burned and the fumes from this went through a big tube to a lead chamber in the acid plant. The chamber was 30ft high by 20ft wide, and we sprayed water into

Fisons 40 Range builds up better crops

Only Fisons 40 Range compounds contain exclusive Fisons A-N

Fisons for good farming

76

A special steam-hauled excursion train passes the Fisons plant in June 1964. Demolition of the old Maxwells buildings is in progress. The fireman is holding out the 'token' which allowed him to travel on the single-track line; the signalman is waiting to collect it opposite his box.

it as well, creating sulphuric acid. This acid was run off and directed to another part of the plant called the Den.

It was smelly when we were charging the fires; really smelly then. That's when they used to bring the children in. They used to say – I can't verify it – that when a child got Whooping Cough it was a tiny little worm in the back of their throat – in the windpipe – which caused the cough. They reckoned the fumes

A house, 'Sunnyside', was built in 1890 for the manager of the plant. It was home, at first, to the Barkers and then to the Wilson family. It was demolished sometime in the 1950s.

This photo shows the house and spacious gardens around 1900.

coming when we charged one of the fires killed off the little worm and that was the end of it.

The Phosphate was ground up in the mill and went along a conveyor belt to the Den. The Den was just like a big motor car tyre. It stood about 25ft high. The phosphate and acid was mixed up in a tank with a paddle in it. When it came out it dropped into the 'tyre', which took about four-and-a-half hours to go round. When the mix got to the top it had set; there was a cutter which broke it up into a powder.

The powder would go up an elevator and then tip into a big heap. There was another conveyor in the top which could move it to different parts of the plant. Underneath the shed where the phosphate was made was another conveyor which brought it and fed it over a set of elevators up onto another conveyor and across the works into a mill. It used to go through that mill and be put into bags. In the early days, we used all hand sewn bags. When we went onto paper, a sewing machine just stitched it across. That was the superphosphate – it was used for fertilizer.

This big wheel, the Den – it was invented by Arthur Wilson, who was works manager at the time. He invented it and Pratchitts of Carlisle made it. It was running very well, and they decided to market it. Well, there was a Japanese firm got interested in it. And another went to a place on one of the Islands in the Thames estuary – I forget which one. Only two were sold I think.

Copper sulphate

Independent of the fertilizer, there was a copper sulphate plant. In there was another furnace for melting the copper, it came out in thin shells and was run off into water. We had a big tower, about 60 feet high; we filled the huge chamber with the Copper Sulphate shells and then filled it with sulphuric acid. Steam was injected into this mix from a boiler there. Once the sulphate had dissolved, it was run off as a liquid into big tanks. The tanks had strips of lead hanging in them from bars above. The Copper Sulphate would crystallise on them – to look at, they were just like blue diamonds!

Market

We sent a lot of superphosphate to the Isle of Man every year. At that time, the 'Assaroe' was running and she took some every week in the season. We also used little boats, 500 ton ones, that could get into Douglas harbour. They used to say we were lifting the Isle of Man a foot higher out of the water every year!

We used to export the Copper Sulphate powder to the Middle East. They used it to spray grapes with. We sent a lot to Greece too, it all went in barrels.

A lot of the fertilizer we produced went into Southern Scotland. A few farmers there had regular accounts and bought a lot from us. It was all road transport – straight to the farms. One morning I came down to work at Silloth, it was before the price was due to go up. There were thirty-four lorries waiting to load! What I did, I told them you'll have to help yourselves if you want to get away, so I gave them positions to get the stuff from and when they got it, to come back to the office to let me check it. In one day we sent over 800 tons out of the place, which was marvellous for the few men we had at the time. I had a call from Head office at Felixstowe, asking how we managed it".

A Fisons works outing in the 1950s. The coach is standing outside the works.
Note the fancy brick-work, this part of the plant dated from Maxwell's original building.

78

The fizzy drinks factory

In 1892, William Crabb, proprietor of one of the town's two chemical works, founded The Silloth Mineral Water Company. The enterprise started off in part of his fertilizer factory.

When Maxwells bought the chemical works, the drinks operation moved to a new site behind Beaconsfield Terrace in West Silloth. Crabb sold the business to Twentyman Irving in 1905. Then, in 1908, William Arnison bought it. Arnison had worked for William Crabb but then left to start his own mineral water business in Wigton.

The Lemonade works at West Silloth

He took over the Silloth works and made bottled drinks there for the next thirty years. Arnisons became a well-known name, supplying a variety of soft and carbonated beverages throughout north Cumberland. The Silloth works closed around 1940, but Arnisons used the premises to distribute their products for a few more years. In 1980, the local press reported that the firm had been sold to Curries of Auchinlek.

An early advert for Crabb's new enterprise showing the lean-to building at his chemical works in which it was originally located.

Gas Supplies

On the Solway Plain, gas was only available in Silloth for most of the century. The gas works there was run initially by the railway company and later by the local council. Coal was burnt to produce the gas, which was then piped to light homes and streets. In the 1920s, the works was modernised and a new gasholder built. Demand increased as gas cookers replaced coal burning ranges.

By the 1950s, gas was no longer made at Silloth. Instead, a large gas works at Carlisle, together with the coke ovens at Workington, fed gas into a series of mains which linked most of the Cumberland towns. This system, managed by the Northern Gas Board from 1949, continued until the arrival of natural gas in new pipelines from the North Sea in the 1970s.

Silloth's disused gasworks was demolished in the 1980s.

The Flour Mills

The Mills of Carr & Co. dominate the dockside at Silloth. On the left is the bulk grain silo erected in 1905. The picture was taken in July 1911 when the barque Invercauld was delivering wheat from Australia.

Throughout the twentieth century, one structure has dominated the Solway Plain. Messrs Carrs flour and feed mills have stood there since the 1880s and are, perhaps, the most recognisable landmark in the area. They are as synonymous with Silloth as the green and the prom.

Carrs had imported wheat into Silloth since the earliest days of the port, but it was not until 1886 that they erected a milling plant at Silloth to process the grain. In the 1870s, the mass cultivation of wheat in North America began. Being better for bread making, it was imported in large quantities to the UK, devastating the British corn market. Industrial mills at ports received the wheat from ships and replaced small country corn mills.

The Silloth mill went into production in 1887 using wheat from many parts of the world. In 1904-5 the factory underwent a major refit. The floorspace was increased and new machinery was installed including a steam engine made by Carel in Belgium. However the most noticeable change was the erection of a huge storage silo which stood next to the mill and whose height made it visible for miles. Over the years, this feature has drawn attention to the presence of the factory and it has been painted many colours, from dark brown to bright green!

Carrs sourced their wheat from all over the world. Australian, American, Russian and European grain arrived at the plant by sea. At first, the sacks of grain were taken off the ships by two cranes.

Then, in 1914, a vacuum suction plant was installed to suck loose, bulk, wheat out of the ships and into the silos. This system was used for the next ninety years. By the 1920s, most ocean-going grain ships

This photo, from 1905, shows the villa that stood next to the mill for many years. It was originally the Manager's House but was later used as offices.

The Steam Engine

were too large to dock directly at Silloth. Instead, wheat was trans-shipped onto coasters at Liverpool or Belfast. During the 1960s and 70s much arrived from France and Holland. Wheat from English farms has long been used as well. Although the basic milling process remained the same, the factory changed a lot. In 1973, an oil fired electric generator was installed and the steam engine was no longer used. The system of drive belts disappeared together with the tall chimney which had been a prominent feature of the works.

Manual tasks were reduced as equipment was automated. By the 1990s, all production could be controlled from electronic panels in booths on each floor. New equipment contained the dust which once floated around the factory and this made a big difference to the working environment. The workforce was reduced to around fifty people by the end of the century. Generations of Silloth families had worked at Carrs. At one point around three hundred people had been employed.

Apprentices were taken on regularly; many a Silloth lad and lass began their working life there. The mill took girls as flour packers. The boys began by sweeping dust off the floors. Sons followed fathers, working their way up to senior responsibilities.

However, as modernization took place, the old days were not forgotten. After the steam engine was retired, it was preserved and remains in place, a magnificent reminder of the age of steam. The engine house became a museum with many interesting exhibits and a display of photographs.

The mills and dock in 1960.

Production

Different varieties of wheat are conveyed from the storage silos and fed through a series of rollers which gradually reduce it to a variety of different flours: plain, brown, malt, etc.

For many years, Carrs produced their 'CC' (Carrs Celebrated) brand of flour. In 1910 their other brands included 'Gold Leaf', 'Bakers Fancy', 'Sunflower', and 'Solway Cream'. Their 'Snowdrop' flour could be bought in the 1920s and, in the 1950s and 60s, the 'Solray' brand was a household name locally.

As well as serving domestic users, a great deal of the flour was sold to large bread and confectionery makers as well as Carrs biscuit factory in Carlisle. Flour was originally transported by rail but, by 1930s, motor lorries laden with the sacks were leaving Silloth daily. By the late 1960s flour was being carried in bulk tankers and Carrs had a sizeable fleet of vehicles.

The Chief

Thomas James Steele was born into a farming family at Wolsty Hall. After working on the farm for a few years, he took a job at Carr's Flour Mill in Silloth. His main responsibility was looking after the magnificent steam engine which powered the entire plant.

He became known throughout the factory as 'The Chief'. Even the boss, Ivan Carr, called him that! He was the chairman of the local branch of the Transport and General Workers Union for around fifteen years, during which time, 100% Union membership was achieved at the mill.

He formed a 'Sick Club' at the plant and founded the Solway Mills Sports Club. In his youth he had been a keen Rugby Union player and, later in life, was in regular demand as a referee for the game.

Thomas Steele and his dog, Gyp.

Tom Steele presiding over a meeting at Carr's mill. At the table, left to right, Harold Stamper, Tom, Mr Scott (Mill Manager), Mrs Scott, Mr Sorrell and Aggie Selkirk.

Tom died at the age of 62 in 1952. In a letter of condolence to his family, Ivan Carr described him as "one of my best friends down at Silloth . . . it was always a pleasure to have a chat with him." This was a quite remarkable tribute from the chairman of a company to its principal union organiser.

Animal feeds

An animal feed plant was built in 1955. Over the years, this became as important a business as the flour milling. Carrs merged with Pattinsons of Whitehaven in a joint venture, supplying a range of solid and liquid feeds.

In 1963, a modern computerised plant was opened, which could make different blends and compounds of animal feed with the press of a few buttons. Products left the plant for farms and merchants all over the North of England and Scotland. This gave work to a number of local hauliers. Output increased but, in the late 1990s, new government regulations came into force. These prohibited such manufacturing operations being sited in residential areas. The plant had to close and demolition took place in 1998.

Left: *Tanker delivering bulk foodstuffs to a farm in the 1960s.*

Right: *Inside the plant. Joseph Hodgson (Works Foreman), William Millican (Press Operator) and Ivan Wallace (Supervisor) are standing beside the press which made the pellets and nuts of animal feed.*

Right: *Demolition of the animal feed plant.*

Sand and Gravel

Civil engineers Costains Ltd using sand from Blitterlees banks, 1940s.

Robert Pigg (right) was one of many local men who worked on the construction of the new sea wall.

The geology of the Solway Plain means that it holds abundant reserves of sand and gravel. This has been extracted in many places over the years, both informally and in designated quarry sites. The land around Westnewton has been particularly used and large amounts were taken from Mawbray banks up until the 1960s. Blitterlees banks also saw extensive quarrying for the construction of Silloth aerodrome and the sea wall.

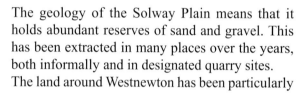

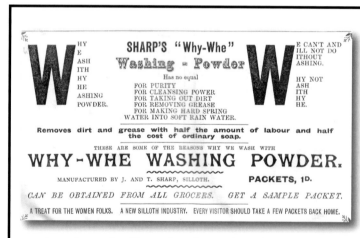

The Sharp family came from Bowness and moved to Silloth in the 1870s. Edward Sharp was a mariner, but his two sons left their mark in other ways. During the 1890s, James and Thomas Sharp set up a fancy goods store on Criffel Street next to the Solway Hotel.

Then they gave it up to start on a new venture – they invented their own washing powder!

An advert the Sharp brothers placed in the 1899 Silloth visitor guide.

In premises at Greenrow, they produced, from a unique recipe, a cheaper and more efficient form of soap to which they gave the clever and catchy name "Why-Whe Washing Powder". Established in 1898, the business ran until the early years of the twentieth century.

This advert and the line in the 1901 census which describes James as "Manager of a dry soap manufactory" are the only records of this extraordinary local enterprise.

After the operation ceased, about 1905, James became a photographer and continued to live, along with the family, on Lawn Terrace.

The Utilities

The twentieth century brought new services to the Solway Plain which changed lives – however it was a gradual process. In 1900 homes were lit mainly by oil lamps and candles, except in Silloth where a Gas Works burnt coal to provide street and domestic lighting. Water came from wells, and waste went into earth closets.

Water

On Boxing Day 1903, Silloth got its first supplies of piped mains water. Until then residents, and even visitors at the smartest hotel, relied on pumps and wells. The Aspatria and Silloth District Water Board had been established a few years earlier to bring a clean reliable water supply, at a time when public health was still a high concern. To provide the supplies, the board dammed the head waters of the River Ellen near Ireby. This process created a new lake - Overwater as well as the Chapelhouse reservoir. Within five years, the scheme was extended with a new main supplying Westnewton and Allonby. More than twenty miles of trunk piping brought water to 10,000 people. The average daily consumption was about 430,000 gallons (almost two million litres). At first, there were problems with the supply becoming discoloured through the presence of vegetable matter in the water. This was solved by the construction of a covered reservoir and filtration plant at Quarry Hill, near Mealsgate. These works, together with a manager's house, opened in May 1913 at a cost of almost £11,000. The new plant could deal with more than 600,000 gallons per day. The water was filtered through sand brought from Leighton-Buzzard in Bedfordshire and lime solution was added to complete the purification process.

In the 1930s mains water was extended to the rest of the area. The 'Holme Parishes Water Scheme' involved laying thirty-five miles of piping from the existing trunk main to serve homes from Salta in the South to Seaville in the North, and Aldoth and Abbeytown in the East.

Work began in April 1935 and was completed the following March. The local board wanted to make maximum use of local labour at a time when many men were looking for employment. The Clydeside Construction Company was awarded the contract. Although not a local firm, they hired local labourers for the job and did not use mechanical excavators. Although they laid the pipes, it was up to each householder to connect up to the new branch mains, which usually followed the local roads. This meant plenty of work for local plumbers! By the end of 1936, most farms and homes had piped water, though there were a few teething problems with flow and quality which took a while to sort out. The Aspatria & Silloth water board continued to improve and maintain the system until water services were nationalised in 1949.

A gathering on Silloth green in 1911 to celebrate the unveiling of the new water fountain.

Members of the board, 1913.

Aspatria Silloth & District
Joint Water Board.

Officers @ Members, 1913.

CHAIRMAN :—MR. JOHN SOUTHWARD,
Kirkland Green.
VICE-CHAIRMAN :—MR. DANIEL DIXON, J. P.
Tarnside, Abbey Town.
MR. ROBERT BELL, Aspatria.
MR. F. GRAINGER, J. P.
Southerfield, Abbey Town.
MR. CHAS. HAWKINS, Silloth.
MR. WILLIAM IRVING, Silloth.
MR. THOMAS OSTLE, Aspatria.
MR. HENRY STODDART, Aspatria.
MR. THOMAS WATSON, Aspatria.
ENGINEER :—MR. JOS. GRAHAM,
28 Castle, St. Carlisle.
MANAGER :—MR. JOHN FERGUSON,
Quarry Hill, Mealgate.
CLERK :—MR. F. RICHARDSON, Solicitor, Aspatria.

Water Board Offices,
Bank Chambers, Aspatria.

Water Crisis!

Just as residents were getting used to turning on taps, unforeseen issues arose!

In 1938, work began on a large RAF base at Silloth. Water was needed on site and it was connected to the main. As construction progressed, more was needed and, once operational, it consumed even more. On top of this, army and RAF hutment camps were unofficially connected to the main. As a result, demand exceeded what could be pumped from the reservoir. Pressure dropped, causing domestic supplies to fail on many occasions. Silloth docks were affected too. It relied on freshwater for the hydraulic system which opened the dock gates and powered cranes and other equipment.

The weather at the time made matters worse. The summer of 1939 was one of the driest remembered, and there were also prolonged droughts in the following years. In between, there were freezing winters with heavy downpours in the hills. These washed silt and stones into the filters and channels. The water board struggled to keep the system working and, after a lot of discussion, the Air Ministry agreed to bear the cost of installing new, larger, pumps to meet demand. In 1942, this emergency 'booster plant' was installed at Quarry Hill in difficult conditions due to manpower and resource shortages.

The new pumps eased the situation but, as consumption continued to rise, another problem occurred. The filtration plant failed and had to be replaced. Residents were getting impure water and, to prevent a health crisis, a works was built to release chlorine into the water. This time no government money was available while manpower and materials were in short supply. The board did what they could in the circumstances and eventually succeeded in restoring the filters.

For much of the war, many local people had to make do with less water as well as less food!

Drains

Drainage systems were provided in SIlloth when the town was built, but the rural area relied on earth closets until sewers were laid in phases from the 1930s on. Sewers had been extended to Skinburness and Blitterlees by 1920. Abbeytown was given proper sewerage in 1938, but Beckfoot and Mawbray were still relying on septic tanks at the end of the century.

At Allonby, residents used the beck flowing through the village to dispose of waste until the council provided drains. In the 1930s one of John Tocher's many jobs was to periodically flush the sewer.

A group of men working on the water scheme supplying the rural areas in 1935.

Electricity

In 1934, mains electricity arrived in Holm Cultram. Before then, the flour mill and the chemical works at Silloth both had their own generators which had been lighting their plants for some years. Passengers on the 'Yarrow' could also experience the novelty of electric lights.

Electricity was heralded as safe, clean and efficient, and the government aimed to give access to all.

Willowholme Power Station, Carlisle.

In 1930, the mid Cumberland Electricity Company was formed with the task of rolling out supplies to the area west of Carlisle. It was one of many such companies set up through a government order at the time. In 1927, a new power station had been opened in Carlisle and pylons took the supply in different directions from there. A new substation was built outside Wigton to tap the power from the main line to West Cumberland and distribute it to local towns and villages by wires on wooden poles.

By January 1934, the wires had reached Abbeytown which, at that time, had yet to have a mains water supply or drains. In March that year, local councillor H J Smith officially opened and switched on Silloth's substation.

As always, there was a mixed response to this new venture. Some residents eagerly wired their homes ready for the coming of the lines. Others had no interest and saw it as an unnecessary extra expense. Aspatria UDC voted to continue using gas for street lighting.

At that time domestic use was limited to lighting and perhaps an electric cooker. Farmers could now use one of the new milking machines. The project was delayed because some landowners objected to the poles and wires going across their estates. There were complaints from residents at the slow progress of the scheme. The wires reached Allonby from Cockermouth later that year and gradually other places were connected. The process of wiring all but stopped during the war, but continued afterwards. The progress made after 1948 was under the newly formed Northwestern Electricity Board. A line to Mealo was begun in 1949, Mawbray had electric by the mid-1950s. It was not until the 1960s that all outlying farms received their supply.

During the 1960s, much of the system was renewed. As more machines and devices were developed, consumption rose. People installed additional circuits and more sockets in their homes. This and complete re-wiring gave work to local electricians for the rest of the century.

SKINBURNESS

TOWER HOTEL

First-Class Hotel in own Grounds
Hot and Cold Water in all Bedrooms
Electric Light :: :: Garage
————Excellent Cuisine————

"*The most comfortable Hotel on the Coast*"

For Terms : Apply Proprietrix   Telephone : Silloth 133

*As late as 1948, when this advert appeared in the Silloth guide,
local hotels were still billing electricity as a luxury item.*

Helen Nattrass remembers . . .

Living on a farm, down a lane, my brother Jack and I had no friends living near and had to amuse ourselves. After doing the daily chores, like feeding hens and gathering eggs, fetching the cows from the fields for milking, filling the coal bucket and gathering kindling from around the farm and hedgerows, we were left to play. Lighting in the country was by oil lamp but we had a battery-operated radio which was listened to for news of the war and "Music While You Work".

Dad was a very clever man and decided he would try and make electricity. He shaped a long piece of wood into a propeller and then acquired some second-hand motor car batteries and a dynamo from a bus, as well as some long lengths of electric cable, probably from the areas near Silloth where the aerodrome scrap was dumped.

With help from the hired man, this propeller was fixed to the Dutch barn, the highest point on the farm to catch the prevailing wind. The thick cable led, from the dynamo, down to the ground and into a small lean-to shed where the batteries were lined up on shelves. From these batteries, another cable was fixed along the buildings, into the house, across the ceiling via the hooks and finished with a single bulb. What excitement when we switched on and had a light!

There was a downside because the batteries were all past their best and would not hold the charge. We had good, white light when the wind blew strongly and, when it didn't, a poor, yellow one

which surged in time with the propeller going round. Dad was way ahead of his time.

During all this work, Jack and I were very industrious, making our own propellers out of scrap wood. From a straight-grained length of 4"x6" wood, we shaped and pared our propellers. We used a pocket knife and steel kitchen knives, which we sharpened on the sandstone steps, copying mother who sharpened the carving knife this way. It was a long process and kept us very busy but, eventually, we could hammer a nail through the centre and fix our propeller to a long stick.

To make the hole bigger and freer we burned it, using one of mother's steel knitting needles plunged into the fire till it was red-hot. Mother was not pleased.

Some windmills were good, some were out of balance or split and then we started again. We ran round the farmyard and then had the bright idea of fixing them to our bicycle handlebars with John Robert string and cycling, as fast as our legs would go, up and down the lane. The "Whizz" was our reward for the hard graft – wonderful! No thoughts of Health and Safety and I can't remember us cutting ourselves – just falling off our cycles.

Later, when an engine driven milking machine was installed, the lighting was also driven by its generator and we could have other equipment: deep freeze, washing machine, etc. The windmill was redundant and taken down. For the Queen's coronation, we could watch the ceremony on TV and this was our entry into the modern world.

Helen's family, the Pearsons, on their farm at Plasket Lands.

CHAPTER SIX

1939 – 1945, The Second World War

War graves and aircraft hangars at Causewayhead.

The Second World War changed the look of this little corner of England for ever. Three large airfields were built – at Silloth, Kirkbride and, further north, at Anthorn. Their runways and many of the buildings remain – as much a part of the landscape as the farms and the sea banks.

Work began on the aerodrome at Silloth in 1938. It was planned as a maintenance and training centre, the site being chosen because of its remoteness from what were expected to be the main operational airfields further south. In April 1940, the No. 1 Operational Training Unit of Coastal Command was established there. Its job was to train bomber crews and the Lockheed Hudson was the plane chiefly used for this work. A bombing range was built on the sea banks near Mawbray. Low flying exercises took place over the Solway, using targets placed in the water, and gunners trained using drogues, huge windsocks, towed by old Fairey Battle bombers.

A Maintenance Unit (22MU) was also based on the airfield. This handled many different kinds of aircraft. The unit fitted radio sets, cannon and machine guns and adapted planes for use in the tropics; civilian technicians carried out this work.

An experienced pilot tested each plane before it was handed over to the Air Transport Auxiliary who flew them on to the operational squadrons. By 1941, there were over 750 civilians, 11 RAF Officers and 19 airmen permanently based in the M.U.

In addition, there was a continuous stream of young men, most in their early twenties, who passed through the base for training. They came, not only from the United Kingdom, but from all parts of the Commonwealth. One of them was John 'Lofty' Gullen.

Lofty arrived at Silloth in April 1942; he turned twenty the following month. Several of the other lads who arrived in the same batch would later serve as his crew. Amongst these was John 'Baptiste' Rutherford from Winnipeg in Canada. He was three years older than Lofty and had been serving in the Canadian Air Force since 1940.

Lofty's first Operational flight was as co-pilot on a Flying Fortress in an Anti-Submarine Patrol, then he was given his own crew and command of a Hudson.

After completing their training at Silloth in July 1942, the crew were posted to Benbecula in

Lofty

the Hebrides where they stayed for a year 'riding shotgun' on the Atlantic convoys.

Lofty was promoted to Flight Lieutenant in 1945. After the war, he set up an engineering business and started to fly again in 1958. He bought a Percival Prentice and kept it until 1972 when it was purchased by the Shuttleworth collection. He died in 1994.

Rutherford returned to Canada and left the RCAF in May 1945 with the rank of Pilot Officer. Sgt S.L Clemson went on to serve on Flying Fortresses in the Bahamas.

All of Lofty's crew survived the war. Sadly, many of the other lads who came to Silloth for their training did not. During the early years of the war, there was an alarmingly high casualty rate amongst them.

By the end of 1942, seventeen Hudsons and one Oxford Bomber had crashed; three more were lost at sea. Fifty-six members of their crews are buried at Causewayhead, many more bodies were never recovered. In March 1943, the Coastal Command

The crew, with their Hudson on the Causewayhead side of the airfield.
(left to right) Rutherford (Navigator), Harvey (Wireless Operator),
Gullen (Pilot) and Clemson (Gunner).

The rather fuzzy snap shows the crew at their later billet on Benbecula together with landlady, Mrs Lee.

The lads outside their hut at West Silloth in 1942. We think perhaps they (and the photographer) had been out on the town for a few jars to celebrate Lofty getting his wings!

Training Unit was moved to Thornaby in North Yorkshire, by which time they had lost a total of sixty aircraft in flying accidents at Silloth. A new command then took over the training operations and units of airmen from Polish and Czech squadrons arrived. Wellington bombers replaced the Hudsons in the skies over Silloth.

During the desert campaigns in North Africa, the Maintenance Unit prepared Hawker Hurricane fighters for action there. Desert camouflage was applied, guns were fitted and harmonised and engines and instruments all fully tested. However, the MU's busiest time came in the build-up to D-Day when, at one point, 740 aircraft were held at Silloth.

Training operations ceased in July 1945 and the airfield then became purely a maintenance unit although its land and buildings were to continue playing an important part in Silloth's story for the whole second half of the century.

Hudson trainer over Grune Point and **(Below)** *on the ground at Silloth,*

So many of these aircraft were lost that The Solway became known locally as 'Hudson's Bay.'

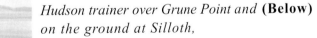

No 6 (Hudson) Operational Training Course, Silloth June 1941.

Third from left, back row, is Eric Crowe who died in December 1942 when his plane was lost over the Atlantic during a patrol from Benbecula.

Romance in the air....

John Jameson, a young South African pilot was stationed at Silloth. During his time there, he met a nineteen-year-old girl from Maryport called Iris. Romance blossomed, they started to go out together and, eventually, got engaged. Telegrams were often sent by John:

"Iris, cancel tonight. Flying".

The telegrams and letters were 'vetted' in case of information getting into the wrong hands.

Sadly, John was killed on a mission. Iris kept all his letters and telegrams for the rest of her life. They were destroyed on her instruction after her death.

Blackout

Right from the start, a news blackout seems to have been imposed on all operations around Silloth airfield. In 1938, when building operations began, the only indication of these in the local press is a report on a Parish Council meeting which gave permission for the "RAF Workers" to use the tennis courts on Sundays.

The news blackout didn't fool the Germans for one minute. The evidence of that can be found on the page opposite. . . .

Luftwaffe reconnaissance photo of the airfield, dated February 1941.

The Silloth Trainer

During the early years of the war, Wing Commander Gordon Butler Iles developed one of the world's first flight simulators at Silloth

In Civvy Street, the Wing Commander worked for the Aeolian Company which manufactured Pianolas. The company got into financial difficulties in 1938 and he left to join the RAF. Here he utilised his expertise in the manufacture of automatic pianos to design a machine which used pneumatics to simulate the conditions the crew would encounter when flying.

It was used primarily for learning drills and handling malfunctions. As well as the basic flying behaviour, it simulated all the engine, electric and hydraulic systems. The control panel, visible in the photo, monitored the crew and allowed the instructor to insert faults for them to deal with.

The first Silloth trainer was designed for the Hudson bomber and, when properly adjusted, gave very realistic responses. Silloth trainers were manufactured for several other types of aircraft during the war and, by mid-1945, 14 of them were in existence or on order but all development ceased in 1946. The RAF Museum at Hendon has a copy of the original manual for the trainer.

Two Navy Men

John Creighton

John Creighton was the son of Thomas and Mary Margaret Creighton of Beckfoot and the husband of Sarah. He was attached to H.M.S. President III, a shore-based establishment in Bristol, which trained seamen for service on defensively equipped merchant ships. He was killed on March 16th, 1943 while serving as a gunner on merchant ship in an Atlantic Convoy which was attacked by a German U-boat Wolf pack. He was 34.

Bill 'Tacky' Richardson

Bill 'Tacky' Richardson came from a naval family. His father, William Gibson Richardson, had served in the First World War; his story is told in Chapter Two.

Bill and his three brothers all joined the Royal Navy. He saw action, firstly on the Atlantic convoys, and then in the Pacific. After facing the horror of the Kamikaze Pilots targeting the ships, he was assigned the awful task of bringing home British prisoners from the Japanese camps.

The movie "*A Yank in the RAF*" came out in September 1941, some months before America entered the war. Tyrone Power plays an American pilot who gets a job ferrying bombers from Canada to England. In London, he meets an old flame, Betty Grable, who is working as a show-girl in the West End. He joins the R.A.F. to impress her and becomes a bomber pilot. Later, he is transferred to a fighter squadron and takes part in the evacuation of allied troops from Dunkirk. **Many of the flying sequences were filmed at Silloth although the contributions of the big Hollywood stars were obviously filmed in the studios there.**

IMAGES © TWENTIETH CENTURY-FOX

Silloth port in the 1940s

Silloth docks were extremely busy as a result of the war. In the late 1930s, the port handled many imports of cement powder from London which was used to build the structures and runways of the aerodrome. Then, in addition to the usual traffic, it was identified by the Government as a safe strategic location for handling military supplies and also coal.

All coal exports to Ireland from the ports in north-east England were diverted to the west coast via the Newcastle-Carlisle railway and then to ports in Cumberland. This was done to protect the trade from German activity in the North Sea and English Channel. All the west Cumberland ports handled this coal, but Silloth saw the greatest increase in traffic.

The docks were chosen as a safe route for sending supplies to the areas of conflict. This included various cargo classed as 'Stores under seal'. Even the port log books do not reveal what this actually was! However, it is now known that the bulk of this classified traffic was in fact barrels and jerry cans of fuel for army vehicles and planes.

Although most of the ships involved were small coasters, a number of ocean going vessels called to load Government stores. The largest ship to visit Silloth during the war was the 'Prince de Liege' which loaded 2,500 tons of cased petrol for Algiers in North Africa.

All this had a huge effect on the port; arrivals jumped from around 20 ships a month in 1939 to between 80 and 100 a month from 1940. This level was maintained until 1947.

The busiest point occurred in April 1943 when there were fourteen ships in dock together, all but one were to load coal for Ireland. This meant berthing two or three abreast and it was a hectic time for the pilots and stevedores who worked day and night. Overtime pay meant some of them brought home a lot of money during the war.

SHIPPING AT SILLOTH	
MONTH	ARRIVALS
Sept 1941	97
May 1942	107
Aug 1942	120
Oct 1942	92
Mar 1943	95
Jul 1943	122
May 1945	68
Oct 1945	85
Jun 1946	74
Sept 1946	84
May 1947	75
Aug 1947	74
Aug 1948	39

Source: Port Records

WARTIME MEMORIES

The late Eric Laws

I was in Silloth all through the war, working first for Maxwell's and then for Fisons at the chemical works. The town was under military rule and you needed a pass to go nearly anywhere. You couldn't go near the railway and, all around the airfield, there were manned check-points.

There was one man shot on Skinburness Road. He didn't stop at the post for the soldiers. Just one bullet and that was it – they shot him. He wasn't a local man, I didn't know him. (Other sources suggest he was a visiting officer). A farmer bought the car he was in to carry pig swill from the RAF mess to his farm to feed the pigs. They never mended the hole in the car, it was there for everybody to see.

I was in the Observer Corps – you had to do something in your spare time. We had a post near the Convalescent Home where there were big banks, we were on top of one of them – you had a good view. We saw some funny things. One

One of the passes issued to local residents.

Sunday evening, I was on the post and there were three WAAFs came along. I don't know where they came from. They came past us, we were covered in camouflage – they couldn't see us. They didn't go twenty yards before they all went down and had a good wee! I couldn't help it – I shouted "Are you feeling any easier?"

There was a fair bit of sex. I can't tell you everything that happened. I don't think there was any organised prostitution in the town – it was just casual stuff. There were girls who used to go down to the docks, you know. They got on the boats where they shouldn't have been.

The Observer Corps Silloth Post

The Golf Hotel was full of WAAFs, I think there were some in the Queens too. I don't think they used the Skinburness, there were gun posts there, one where you turn to go onto the marsh and one just through Calvo. You weren't free to just wander about. When we were on the post we had rifles and were supposed to challenge anybody who came along.

Once, somebody climbed up Christ Church steeple and tied a pair of WAAF's knickers on the top. It was Alex Ramsey, one of the lads who were drowned at Skinburness trying to save the wildfowlers. He worked at the garage – he was a damn good mechanic.

In the war, the docks were full from side to side. They used to export an awful lot of fuel. It came into Carlisle and came down in railway wagons. It was petrol in barrels and jerry cans. I remember Tommy Daley, a shunter, telling me he had gone to Carlisle to pick up a load of 45 wagons. It was a hell of a night and he was supposed to go back for another load. So he hooked both loads together. Coming into Kirkbride, there's a slight incline; he said to the driver, you'll have to get your speed up or we'll never get over that bank. They got over – but just. They had ninety wagons loaded on all full of petrol cans!

A lot of the petrol went to Malta for the forces; the boats that went out joined up in convoys. You never heard anything more about them – whether they got through or not. They were just small coasters 500 to 1000 tons.

A lot of coal went out of the docks too – to Ireland – it was loaded by the coal hoist at the east end of the dock. When the war ended, they drained the dock and took hundreds of tons of coal out of it. There was ammunition went out too. I think some of the ships went round the Cape of Good Hope.

I remember the plane crashes in the Solway; Coastal Command used to operate out of Silloth. When they started the 1000 bomber raids, a lot of planes went out of Silloth. You could see 50 or 60 planes in the air at once in our (Observer Corps) area – it took some doing to keep your eyes on them all.

At the chemical works during the war labour was bad to get. There was a POW camp at Kingside full of Italians. So we negotiated to get some of them to work. There were eighty came in a huge bus; when they got out they were like a load of monkeys chattering. I had such a job with them. There was one called Jacobini he was cook – he just had a brazier and used to bring the ingredients from the camp. The smells he made were wonderful. He brought me a lot of phrase books and I set to work and learned the language. At first, I found one man who knew a bit of English and I used to get him to translate for me but I would tell the men to do something and he would tell them to do something completely different. When things got easier, we

Four Silloth lads. (left to right): *Alex Ramsey, Edwin Walton (Coalman), George Clowes and Alex Moor. Alex Ramsey is mentioned in Eric's story.*

started to get our own men back and lost the Italians but then they sent us some Germans. The manager said you'll have to learn German now! The Germans are supposed to be good workers but give me the Italians. The Germans I found very arrogant and a bit finnicky about doing any work at all.

Pat Antolak

During the war I lived in Allonby where my father was the vicar. I had attended a teacher training college and the headmaster of the Nelson School at Wigton offered me a job there. The school was '*all-boys*' then but so many of the staff had been called-up that they were forced to take on female teachers. I was very happy there.

I had to travel to Wigton and back on the bus. It was difficult, there weren't many buses and I had to change at Silloth and wait there for the next one. Sometimes I would start to walk home after school and hope to hitch-hike. It was much safer in those days than it is now. I often used to get a lift with Greggain's wagons. They were carrying sand from the coast to be made up in bags for the air-raid defences. Very often the cab was full of men and they would say "*Get up, lass*" and I would get into the back of the wagon which was empty of course. It had been full of sand and it was still blowing around in there. I used to get covered in it and had to wash my hair when we got back to Allonby. Sometimes, if it was wet, I wouldn't start to walk and I would go into the Queens Hotel for a cup of tea and I used to mark books in there. Some Canadian Airforce men were billeted there and I didn't get a very good impression of them. I thought they were brash and not very well behaved in the public lounge. They would sprawl around and put their feet on the mantelpiece, I didn't think our boys would have done that.

I wasn't called-up, being in a profession where people were needed but I busied myself with voluntary work as far as I could. After school, I used to go for an hour with the WVS at the Reading Room. We made camouflage nets there to send out to the troops in North Africa. The nets were hung from a big beam across the room. We had to follow a pattern with them – it was mostly sandy colours because they were going to the desert. There were green and brown bits we had to slot in according to the pattern which was stamped on the netting. Sometimes, just for a lark, we girls used to put in little messages for the boys – "Give 'em hell, boys" or something like that!

In the summer holidays, I used to go to Maryport Cottage Hospital as a nursing auxiliary. Matron Campbell was always grateful for a little domestic help on the wards. I scrubbed out lockers and emptied the usual receptacles into the sluice.

Then, of course, we had evacuees sent to Allonby from the North-East. They had to be met at Bulgill station, the nearest railway stop. One day, this big load of mothers and babies came from the Newcastle area. The poor things had been on the train since seven or eight o'clock in the morning. It had been a twelve hour trip for them with the young babies and just what they could carry with them. Some of them had been bombed out. They came to Allonby and I was the WVS Reception Officer for them. I had to welcome them in and see they got to the right place at the right time. When they arrived, there were some nursing mothers who hadn't had anything to drink and they wanted water badly. So I had to ask someone from a nearby farm if we could have one of their milk churns and fill it with water for these poor mothers to have a drink.

Hundreds of evacuated children, mostly from Tyneside, were sheltered in our area throughout the war years. Their story has been told in the previous **Plain People** *books.*

A Cumberland bus of the type in use during the war.

We had quite a number of evacuees in Allonby but they didn't stay long. They had left when things over there were really bad and then they returned. We had a mother and four children at the vicarage. We had an attic with back stairs up to it and they had that like a flat of their own. They had to use our kitchen but they came down the back stairs when they wanted it. They had a sitting room and two bedrooms up in the attic so they were quite comfortable there.

Evacuees at the door of Allonby vicarage.

After a while, when things had settled down a bit, they started to have bus trips for relatives who wanted to come and see their loved ones. They used to descend on Allonby from the North-East on a Sunday which was rather a busy day for a vicar's household to welcome these people in. Anyhow they came and made themselves comfortable with us for the day but they were fairly choosey about what they wanted to eat.

The children went to the village school. It was a difficult time; we used the church hall to get things sorted out. There was no military presence in Allonby but the Silloth boys used to come on their bicycles to the little dances in the village hall and livened-up the village.

Eugeniusz John Antolak

'EJ' was born in Warsaw in 1908. He joined the Polish Air Force and trained as a fighter pilot at the Dęmblin Officer Cadet Flying School. From 1934, he was involved in general duties and then, in 1937, joined the staff at Dęmblin. In 1939, when Germany invaded Poland, he was demobilised along with all other military personnel. He escaped from Poland, posing as a chauffeur, and drove his own car through the Balkans to Greece. Here he took a ship to Marseilles and joined the French Air Force in Lyons.

On the collapse of France, he hid in the hold of a coal ship bound for Falmouth and then reported to the headquarters of the Polish Forces in Blackpool. From there he was posted to a Polish squadron of the RAF and arrived at Silloth in 1941. All Polish Officers joining the RAF were demoted one rank so Kapitan Antolak became a mere Flying Officer.

He acted as a test pilot for the Maintenance Unit on the airfield, checking out the airworthiness of the planes they had prepared for active service.

For relaxation, he used to hire a horse at Jackson's Riding School in Allonby. It was there that he met the vicar's daughter, Pat Hodges. They became engaged and married in April, 1943.

After the war, EJ became involved in the education of adults with mental health problems. In 1993, the couple retired back to Silloth and EJ died there in 1998.

Letters to Canada

William & Mary Marshall   *Harold*

William and Mary Marshall lived at Longwood, Causewayhead right on the edge of the airfield. Throughout the war, they wrote regularly to their nephew, Harold, in Canada who kept all their letters. These extracts show what was on the mind of the local residents at the time.

January 1940

"We hardly knew it was Christmas if we hadn't got a bit goose and the New Year, J.W. brought us a cock chicken and a plum pudding and mother and I had a good tuck-in. Do you know, Harold, in parts of Scotland the people are selling hens for 9d. and they used to be four or five bob*, because they can't possibly get food for them and there are hundreds dying of hunger. We have got our rations nearly one month now – a pound of butter a fortnight so we haven't been putting it on an inch thick. . . . You were asking if there are been any dances this winter. There hasn't been because they put the air force men in the hut as every place is full up with them and the rectory as well as the mission hall and the reading room too. The flying field has been ready for about six months now. It is in Johnny Baird's field along the Silloth road.

When they rise and come down they get mainly right across for Hartlow and sometimes come right over the house so we can see them very plain. They have two big hangars in Johnny's field opposite the church. John's wife looks after the church now and Mr Havel preaches. He comes from Holland and nobody likes him. I don't for one. The Air force have taken Dodd's house at The Wath and they are living down at Blitterlees now. They were very downhearted at having to leave, but that's the government for you. They also took Carter-Woods big place, The Towers, as there was nobody in it after they both died. Cannon Walker is still in bed, he can't walk for his legs. Uncle Willie has three evacuees from Newcastle. When they were evacuated to Silloth he got three and we had two but they have left us and gone back to Newcastle. We get 8/6d. per child for keeping them, of course they were to feed."

*9d equals just under four new pence; a "bob" was one shilling – 5p.

July 1940

"We get the Germans over nearly every night. They dropped one bomb in the cemetery beside the church and blew a few coffins and skulls up.

Another fell behind Polly Timperton's farm and made a big crater. Another fell at Dockray's of Blackdyke it was an incendiary bomb. It burned the buildings down but no damage was done to the house."

Undated letter, late 1940.

"There was a severe accident on the aerodrome a week ago. An aeroplane crashed and killed one man dead out. He was cut in two. There were nine injured and eight have died since. They were all 18. They were as well dead, poor lads, they were mangled to death. There was a plane took fire three weeks ago. It started at 11 at night and burned till 1am. It was an American bomber, it cost £2,300 it is a lot of money, they won't want many like that. . . all the roads to the aerodrome have barriers across and you can't get to Silloth without a pass. There are soldiers on guard all night and day. There are 500 soldiers at Silloth and 1,000 airmen. 1,500 aeroplanes and more coming. We have the WAAFs at Silloth, they look after the airmen. Amy Johnston the fine flyer has been here all summer. I hope Jerry never gets here or we'll all pass off. We have a big dug-out in the orchard they are busy building air-raid shelters at Silloth."

This final extract gives some idea of the rumours which spread in the absence of much official news. Amy Johnston did work for the Air Transport Auxiliary and so it is possible she flew into Silloth at some time before her death in January 1941 but there was never an accident in which eight airmen were killed. A true, eye-witness account of the incident is given by a young airman. . . .

Richard Thomas

We were waiting in the dispersal hut for the aircraft to taxi round and pick us up; ten or twelve of us in full flying kit. The blackness of the night was total. Not a glimmer of light showed across the wide expanse of the airfield. Soon the runway lighting would be switched on for the first aircraft to take off. It was only the second time we had been in-volved in night flying. I could still feel the wobbles in my stomach from the first session. A roar of engines sounded outside. I pulled on my helmet. I barely heard the sergeant's voice shouting above the racket.

"Come on there. Make it snappy. First crew aboard. Second to stand-by."

The man next to me rose to his feet, the pages of a letter clutched in his hand. He moved forward out of the hut, his companion following him. I got up and moved to the doorway, watching the first crew walk out to the waiting aeroplane. My cry of warning was whipped away by the Hudson's slipstream. The second man had moved around in a circle to reach the open door, the first walked straight on, head down.

I sensed the impact as the propeller blade sliced through the thickness of the flying jacket, saw the figure of the man being thrown into the air to land in a crumpled heap on the tarmac. The pages of the letter floated upwards before fluttering down to rest beside the still form. He looked like a rag doll thrown away by a child at the end of a day's play. I felt the gorge rise in my throat, felt the urge to be sick sweeping over me.

"Keep them moving, Sergeant!" A voice sounded from the darkness. "Keep on flying. I'll make arrangements for this to be cleared up. And get that bloody aircraft out of the way." The duty officer sounded distraught. As the first Hudson trundled away, our aircraft came into view. Ray and I skirted round the dead airman. A pool of blood was spreading across the tarmac, looking dark and ominous in the dim light from the dispersal hut. As I came up to where the figure lay I realised that the man's head was detached from the body. The propeller blade had torn through the soft flesh with the precision of an executioner's sword.

The following day Ray asked me, "Do you know what was in the letter that poor devil was reading? It was from a well-meaning neighbour, telling him that his wife was fooling around with some soldier from the local barracks." No doubt the letter had distracted the man at a time when he needed all his wits about him. His death cast a pall of gloom over the remaining weeks of the course.

'George didn't come back' by the Canadian war artist, Miller Brittain.

Richard Thomas recalled his bomber training at Silloth in his autobiographical novel 'Towards the Sun'. These edited extracts give a unique and vivid account of what actually went on at Coastal Command's Operational Training Unit during the early years of the war.

Training at Silloth

Ray Simpson and I arrived at Silloth, a remote outpost on the Cumbrian coast, in the summer of 1940. Two Yorkshire men to be trained as combined wireless operators and gunners aboard Coastal Command's bombers.

The wireless training included transmitting and receiving, checking the equipment and carrying out emergency repairs. We learned to tune the set on fixed and trailing aerials, on HF and VHF bands,

how to check for faults and use the radio compass to obtain a fix on the aircraft's position. Gunnery training took a back seat while there was a new discipline to learn - ASV. The initials stood for Air to Surface Vessel, a device which sent out a signal and received a visual indication of any ship, large or small, for a distance of up to ten miles.

Soon, we were assigned as wireless operators and air gunners to the crew of a Hudson with Pilot Officers Willis Roxburgh, a tall, dark-haired Scotsman with a cultured accent, and John Owen, a small, sandy-haired man with quicksilver reactions and an engaging smile. Both these men had been trained as pilots and had also taken a dead-reckoning course so that they could alternate between flying the aircraft and navigating.

Soon we would be embarking on missions where it would be essential that we could trust each other implicitly. Ray and I knew each other's strengths and weaknesses. The two officers were unknown quantities but they were the men on whom our chances of survival would depend.

I spent my first hour aboard a Hudson in the wireless compartment checking the equipment, and the remainder of the fight in the gun turret. For twenty minutes, I operated the turret, turning it through its maximum swing, raising and lowering the guns. I came out of the aircraft feeling wildly excited. The Americans had provided

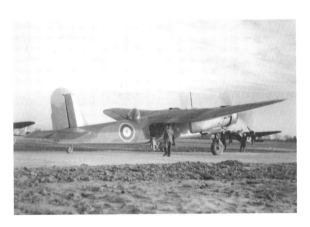

The Blackburn B.26 Botha, a British four-seat reconnaissance and torpedo bomber, entered service with the RAF in 1939 and was used for training at Silloth prior to the arrival of the American Lockheed Hudsons. It was underpowered and was quickly withdrawn from operations.

the RAF with a fine, robust looking aeroplane. It was a good start to our flying careers. Now we had to learn how to use it.

I liked the Lockheed from the moment I climbed up into its bulbous body. There was a feel and a smell to it which was difficult to describe. The wireless operator's cabin was a joy to behold. Shut off from the main body of the aircraft, the radio equipment was set out on a neat rack on the port side, with the ASV set just behind it. For the air-gunner there was the thrill of climbing into the Boulton-Paul turret. It was silky smooth in operation and sported two .303 machine guns. Two side guns were provided for use by the wireless operator in an emergency. And the smell? It was a unique blend of dope, brand new fabrics, and the odour of the Elsan closet, all mixed up with tinges of hydraulic and de-icer fluids, petrol, oil and rubber. The Hudson looked good, smelled good, and flew like a dream.

For two weeks Ray and I took turn-and-turn-about in the wireless compartment and the gun turret. We used wireless and R/T communication. We practised

The Oxford Trainer and its cockpit.

bombing at high and low levels and at periscope height. We trained for air-to-air and air-to-sea firing.

We did navigation exercises on to fishing vessels, controlled descents through clouds, photographic reconnaissance, instrument flying, ASV searching, and we learned how to shut off one engine and keep the aircraft flying on the other.

All the time, we were getting to know each other, smoothing out any possible areas of friction and finding out how to deal with the Officer / NCO relationship both on the ground and in the air. As each day passed the fine tuning took place, each of us beginning to react by instinct to the requirements of the others.

Spare time activities were virtually nil. Silloth had little to offer, nor did the small towns down the coast like Maryport and Workington. Carlisle was the nearest town of any size but neither Ray nor I made any effort to go there. We wrote letters, waited eagerly for each day's mail, talked about the training and discussed ways of improving it, read books and tried to shut out the sound of the cracked gramophone records played over and over again by an enthusiast at the other end of the hut.

Incident with a WAAF

One bright morning in late August, I climbed aboard an Airspeed Oxford and settled down in the wireless compartment. I was surprised to see that the Flight Lieutenant had a passenger. It was a trim figure in blue uniform, with a bob of brown curls showing under the rim of her hat – a WAAF. The girl turned her head, flashing me a smile, as the aircraft taxied out to the end of the runway. I just shrugged my shoulders. I felt sure the flight was not authorised but it was nothing to do with me. As soon as we were airborne, I set to work on the exercise which I had been set. Up to now, I had passed every test. There was no need to think that today would be different.

I was halfway through tapping out a long coded message when I felt a sudden "G" force; the pilot had stood the aircraft on its nose. The dive was long and fast. My hand pressed down on the Morse key, I tried to pull it away but with no effect. I started to sweat as I realised that a long continuous wail of sound would be piercing the eardrums of the operator back at base.

As the Oxford came out of the dive, my hand jumped off the key but the relief was short-lived. The pilot was determined to show off; for ten minutes he threw the training aircraft around the sky like a fighter ace.

Suddenly, I felt the contents of my stomach rise. I had never been sick in the air. This time there was no containing it. After one particularly violent lurch, I heaved. The remains of my breakfast spewed over the wireless set and across the documents spread out in front of it. Never before had I felt so ill.

I was gripping the sides of my seat, staring at the mess around me. Tears were streaming down my face, I was just praying for the nightmare to end. Gradually, the movement of the aircraft returned to normal. Minutes later, we were coming in to land.

When we reached dispersal, I waited for the others to get out. I felt absolutely wretched. The girl passed by, her pretty face registering her disgust; the pilot didn't give me a second glance.

"What sort of a mess is this then?" The Flight Sergeant in charge of the ground crew yelled, peering angrily at the interior of the Oxford.

"You know what you've got to do now? You get a pail of water and a mop and clean up this little lot. I'm not having my lads go in there till it's done. And I mean clean. Pristine in fact, jump to it, sergeant!"

It took a couple of hours of hard work to return the Oxford to its previous condition. Even then a faint odour of sickliness still pervaded the overlying aroma of disinfectant. I had never felt so humiliated. By the time I got back to the hut its occupants were waiting for me. The news had spread round the station like wildfire. Their jibes and frequently offered advice rang in my ears. To rub salt in the wound the Signals Officer marked the exercise with one word - FAILED.

On the following day there was an enquiry into the incident. My version of the events was listened to with some sympathy. So much so that, within a week, the pilot received his marching orders - to the Middle East, some said. It stilled the ribbing from my hut mates but the hurt remained. Of the WAAF there was no sign. Rumour had it that she too had been sent a long, long way from Silloth.

Terry Nave remembers . . .

I married Flying Officer Douglas Nave at Easter, 1945.

What to wear was a real problem; all clothing was rationed. I was working as a nurse so I qualified for a scheme run by the Americans for members of the services. Through the scheme, I obtained a very elaborate gown in Ivory Grosgrain – it was pure Hollywood – I felt very glamorous.

I purloined some clothing coupons from my fiancé and used these to make five dresses for my bridesmaids.

CHAPTER SEVEN

1946 – 1959, The Post-War Years

The Amusements. Local lads (left to right)
Phil Allison, Robert Dalzell, Ian Baty and Bill Allison on the green.

In 1946, England was a grey and cheerless place. In Holme St Cuthbert, the large rural parish between Silloth and Allonby, there was no electric supply. Homes were lit by paraffin lamps and the cattle were still milked by hand.

In Silloth, the streets were lit by gas. The green was dotted with air-raid shelters and barbed wire stretched along the shoreline from the docks to Skinburness Road. The sea defences had been virtually washed away, huge holes had appeared and flooding had uprooted many of the pine trees.

The country was desperately short of food. Almost everything was rationed. The prices farmers received for their produce was regulated by the Ministry of Food. The Women's Land Army and many German and Italian Prisoners of War were still working on local farms. In late July, a 'Holiday Camp' opened in Abbeytown where families from the towns could stay while they helped with the harvest. In October, the children had a week off school for 'Tattie Picking'.

The farmers' families suffered less than the city dwellers from the food shortages. They had supplies of most basic foodstuffs in their fields and yards.

In April 1946, the *West Cumberland Times* reported that the children of Holme St Cuthbert parish had collected fifty-seven dozen eggs and presented them to the Cumberland Infirmary in Carlisle. The patients must have thought this a great treat. Normally, the egg ration was one per person per week. Most families would have been using a dried egg powder; one packet of this could be substituted for the single fresh egg and made up into the equivalent of twelve scrambled eggs.

The main sources of entertainment in these post war years were the cinemas and radio. There were cinemas in Silloth, Aspatria and Wigton plus two in Maryport. Television, picked up from distant transmitters in Scotland and Lancashire, arrived in the early fifties – just in time for the Coronation. Dances, held virtually every weekend, in the local village halls provided the best opportunity for younger people to get together.

It was a period of full-employment and wages, even for farm workers, began to rise. New businesses appeared, agriculture became more mechanised, tourism grew and, finally, the local people's standard of living improved.

Make do and mend

The 'Make Do and Mend' campaign had been introduced by the wartime government in 1943. There was a shortage of imported materials and clothing manufacturers were forced to give priority to making uniforms for the forces. Clothes rationing continued long after peace was declared.

Betty Connolly remembers . . .

Everybody had to make do and mend. New clothes were hard to come by anyhow so most women, if they couldn't already knit and sew, soon learned.

Wool was rationed so old jumpers were unpicked and washed ready to be knitted into new. Old garments were cut up to make rag rugs. Darning wool wasn't rationed so it was bought and carefully hoarded then made up into striped jumpers – it took as long to sew in the ends as it did to knit.

Net curtains could not be bought easily so my mother begged some butter muslin from the butcher. These were carefully washed and made into curtains. She then embroidered dots on each one – very stylish! When the stair carpet started wearing, my mother made yards of carpet pegged with old wool – it lasted years.

My older sisters noticed the confines of clothes rationing more than I did. I was still at school and mother made all my skirts and jumpers cut down from my sisters' cast-offs. By altering garments and decorating them with braid and buttons they could be made to look like a different outfit.

Crochet cotton was used to make dishcloths which, eventually, were used as floor cloths. My eldest sister got married during the war and extra coupons were given for the event. She married in a smart dress and jacket, mindful that it could be used again and again. I would have loved to be a bridesmaid but no coupons could be spared to get me a dress. I wore my Sunday best which had to suffice.

Men's shirt collars, when worn out, were unpicked and turned to last longer. Boys never wore long trousers until they went to senior school. Short trousers with knitted socks were the norm, even in winter.

If you knew anyone who worked where parachutes were packed, sometimes you could get hold of flawed silk – this was wonderful to make up into underwear!

John Nattrass and Alan Osborn.

Isaac Donald, Willie and Davina Rudd, Mrs. Rudd with Jean and Marty Donald at Highlaws.

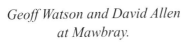

Geoff Watson and David Allen at Mawbray.

The New Look

New sea wall, new promenade and New Look fashions at Silloth.

In June 1947, Christian Dior launched his new fashions and caused a worldwide sensation. The new line was feminine with small, nipped-in waists, billowing skirts and soft, gentle shoulder lines. This 'New Look' signalled a sharp contrast to the austere wartime fashions.

Clothes rationing ended in March 1949 and soon shop window displays began to look exciting and colourful. Market stalls were piled high with new patterned fabrics for the home dressmaker – a great change from 'Make Do and Mend'.

To give the New Look silhouette, underskirts had to be full, they were made from artificial silk (Rayon) or layers of net. Girls dressed for an evening of dancing could hardly walk side-by-side because of these full, swishing skirts.

American Servicemen, stationed here during the war, had first brought nylon stockings – a fashion to die for in the 50s. Nylon was the 'In' material for fashionable clothing and underwear. It was easily laundered and drip-dried over the bath, ready to wear the next day. Sewing machines needed new needles to cope with this new material. It had one big draw-back – too hot an iron and your garment melted or shrivelled-up; you just made this mistake once!

Left:

Teacher, Norah Edgar, shows off the colourful new fabrics in her full skirt while, on the dockside, Ernie Allan of Botcherby models the very latest styles for men.

Above: *Home Perm time!*

Josephine Best (née Darby) remembers. . .

The Palace Ballroom in Maryport held dances every week on Wednesday and Saturday. It cost a shilling on Saturday and sixpence on Wednesday. There was always a dance band, sometimes it might be Ivy Benson, Sid Lawrence or Wee Willie Harris. Occasionally, on a Friday, an Airforce band would play. No alcohol was sold on the premises, just tea, coffee or soft drinks. The men usually went to the local pubs and, when they closed at ten o'clock, came to the Palace to meet their girlfriends.

Dance night in our house was hectic – with four sisters battling to get ready; hair to wash, clothes to iron and legs to tan with gravy browning. Hair was worn up, fastened with a comb or, later, in page-boy style. Make-up was very scarce and, what there was in the shops, was very expensive. Toothpaste was difficult to find so we used salt.

Usually, somebody couldn't find her favourite blouse or jumper or her best shoes. Eventually, the final touch – a black velvet 'choker' worn round the neck, sometimes with the addition of a little brooch. One by one, the sisters left the house in their finery to have a few dances before the boys came back from the pub.

That favourite blouse which had gone missing often turned up – on another sister – during the quick-step. "No wonder I couldn't find it." The reply was always "First up, best dressed!"

Left:

Eva, Josephine, Joyce and Mary Darby

Redmayne's Silloth factory

Redmaynes were an old-established firm of tailors in Wigton. After the war, they opened a factory in Silloth. Production began in the old Arnison's lemonade factory at West Silloth then, in 1948, they moved to premises in Eden Street in the building now used by the Bowling Club. They announced plans to employ up to eighty workers there.

The factory made plastic raincoats, capes for hairdressers and beauty salons, hanging covers to protect clothes from moths and tea cosies. They also manufactured a range of small plastic items such as jam pot covers, shoe bags and Christmas Stockings.

The firm employed high-frequency electronic welding around areas such as button-holes and sleeves but used conventional sewing machines to stitch most of the garments together. The Silloth factory closed around 1970 and production moved to Penrith.

Redmayne Plastic Macs

As one of the pioneers of Plastic Rainwear we are proud to introduce the latest Redmayne Plastic Mac. It is produced in the new "Fabrilon" cloth finish plastic which has a matt surface. All seams are electronically welded. The sleeves are specially cut to hang from the shoulders easily. With new design collar, welded buttonholes and pockets. Roomy yet folds into small space. Mid-Grey Shade **£1.1.0**

Iris Little (née Haughan) remembers . . .

After attending Silloth School, I went on to the Gregg School in Carlisle and then got a job as a typist in the office at Redmaynes. It was a very happy place; there were four or five of us in the office and we were all kept busy with invoices and other jobs.

The factory supervisor was Lilly Bell from Wigton, Harry Gill was the office manager and Erinie Wood was the manager in dispatch downstairs. There were two directors in charge; one was Brian Wigglesworth, who had married Hazel Redmayne. He was killed in a motor accident with his brother. The other director was Mr Cavaghan from Wigton.

They had a big show in London every year. That always brought in a lot of orders for export; I particularly remember sending some stuff off to Cyprus. A lot of the big British stores bought our goods too – John Lewis was a good customer so were Bourne and Hollingsworth, and Kendal's, there were quite a few.

Iris on a works outing with Barbara Grandison.

We had trips every year; usually it was Blackpool and we would have our lunch at R.H.O. Hills who were customers of ours too. Then we had the rest of the day to ourselves. One year we went to Edinburgh for a change. I worked at Redmaynes for about three years and then my family moved to Carlisle.

In the summer of 1951, the whole country let its hair down for a few months to celebrate the Festival of Britain. The main event was an exhibition on London's South Bank which attracted almost eight and a half million visitors during the five months it was open. Many other towns and cities joined in the celebrations. Carlisle organised a vast historical pageant in the shadow of the castle walls.

Along the coast, celebrations were somewhat low-key. Allonby organised a Festival of Antiques in the Reading Room but Silloth went to town with a special carnival week.

Redmayne's prize-winning float celebrated 100 years of beachwear – "From Bloomers to Bikinis". The lorry was decorated with the firm's plastics and the bikinis were also made from plastic at their Silloth factory. The bloomers were hired from a fancy dress firm for the occasion.

The bathing belles are (left to right) Jean Rogerson, Iris Haughan, Edith Richie and Jean Baxter.

The Silloth Squatters

At the end of the war, Britain faced an acute housing shortage. The situation was worse in the big cities where many houses had been destroyed by bombing but it even affected parts of Cumberland. In February 1946, the council estimated that forty-eight families had no house of their own in Silloth. There were two cases of overcrowding and thirty-four new homes were needed to complete their pre-war slum clearance programme.

In August 1946, some of these homeless families took the law into their own hands. They moved into the RAF huts at West Silloth which had been standing empty for almost a year.

John Winter, together with his wife and five young children led the move. They had been living in a small house with two other families. John climbed in through an open window and opened the door for the others. Joe Buchanan's family occupied another room in the hut. He told a *Cumberland News* reporter that he was there to stay, "We are sick to death of furnished rooms where we are not wanted," he said.

Within a week or so, about seventy people were squatting in three separate sites around the area. They formed a committee and collected a weekly 'rent' from each family. This was to be handed over to the owners when the situation was clarified. Wing-Commander Doyle, the local C.O. agreed to turn on the water supply to the huts and to restore the electricity as soon as safety checks were carried out. Some of the families used a boiler house as a communal kitchen but most cooked on the coal-burning heating stoves which stood in each hut.

The locations of the huts used by the squatters are circled on this "revised" O.S. map of 1948. It is something of a curiosity itself. Although the former RAF camps are shown, the airfield itself is completely blanked-out.

Silloth House Farm (top right) had been demolished in 1938. Maybe, by 1948, the government were worried about the Russians finding out the locations of important military installations!

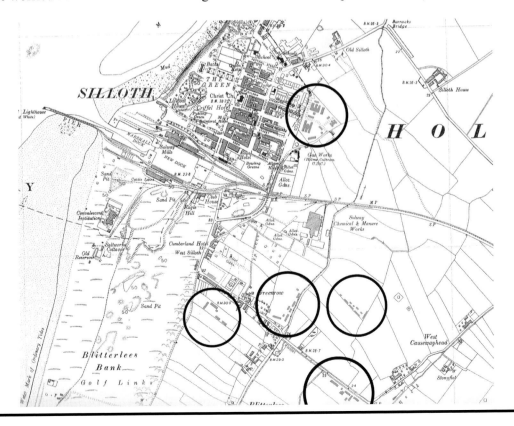

Within a few days of the first families moving-in, a tragedy occurred. Three-year-old Lawrence Piercy, the son of an LNER engine driver, drowned. The boy had gone out to play in the afternoon and had fallen into a thirty-foot square emergency reservoir which contained five feet of water and was surrounded by a barbed wire fence.

They recovered the boy's body in the evening and Dr Barton pronounced him dead at the scene. The coroner later returned a verdict of death by misadventure. He warned the families of the dangers of living on a former military site where they might expect to encounter such dangers and could even find explosives and 'other such things'.

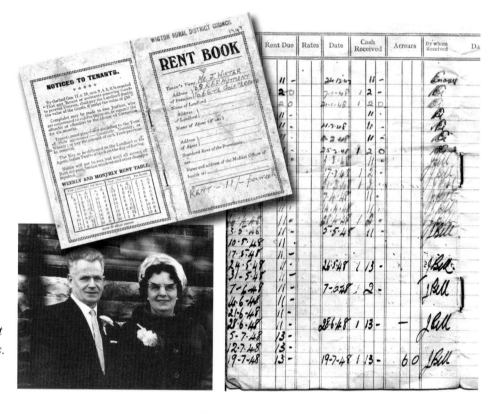

John and Bessie Winter with their rent book, issued by the District Council, after it took over the huts.

In early September, Wilfred Roberts, the local MP, visited the squatters to offer his support. He thought it was "an admirable thing that people should occasionally act on their own and not wait for official decisions." He felt that, with only a little help from the council, the huts could provide as many as forty perfectly satisfactory homes for Silloth people - at very little cost.

Later that month, Mr H Morton, known as the squatters' guardian angel, addressed the Wigton Rural District Council. He asked the council to adopt the huts as temporary dwellings until houses could be built for the families. The clerk told him that negotiations were taking place and a national policy regarding the use of former military camps for housing was under consideration.

The Huts on the site near the gasworks.

Sally Akitt (left) and Mary Taylor outside the huts. Sally was the wife of Stanley Akitt, the fisherman.

In May 1947, the huts were finally transferred to council ownership. By this time, more than thirty families were living there including some from Ireby, Crofton, Maryport, High Harrington and Abbeytown.

Progress on building new houses at The Crofts was painfully slow. The Ministry of Housing strictly controlled the allocation of building materials which were in short supply. In April 1951, the local papers reported that forty houses had been completed and a further twenty-four would be available shortly. The council fixed the rent for the new houses at £1.25 per week, compared to the 55p. which the families had been paying for their huts.

Dr T.S. Jones, the council's medical officer, reported that thirty-nine families were still in huts where conditions were "not fit for human beings." He claimed that, if people had to go on living in them for a few more years, there would be injury to health. "Doctor's surgeries in Silloth are now full on account of people having to live in these hutments," he said. The council agreed that, as families moved out, the huts would be made uninhabitable to avoid problems in the future.

The huts stayed in use as 'Council Houses' until the mid-1950s when the last of the families finally moved to the new 'Crofts' estate nearby.

These members of the Bell and Akitt families were all brought-up in the former RAF huts.

Adults (left to right): *Ethel Akitt, Margaret Bell (nee Akitt), Cyril Akitt, Winnie Akitt and Tommy Bell.* **Children:** *Harry Akitt, Susan Bell, Colin Akitt, Anthony Akitt, Jimmy Bell.*

Tommy and Margaret Bell lived, with their children, in the barracks on what later became Stanwix's Caravan Site. They eventually moved into one of the first houses to be completed on The Crofts. The children had a great time living in the middle of a building site for several years.

Stanley Akitt and his wife Sally, with his brother, Cyril, his wife Ethel and their sister, Mabel Johnson with her husband Albert (Mick) all lived in the huts near the gasworks.

They are pictured here in the garden of the Akitts' parents in Latrigg Street in 1948. The Gasworks huts, known as 'Pennine View', can be seen in the background.

Joan Palmer (née Ostle) remembers . . .

When I was little, at the end of the war, we were living in the old Academy buildings at Greenrow. They had been divided into four houses. The Minnicans lived on the front, then there was a family called Gass and, behind us, the Birketts.

It was a bit overcrowded; as well as my parents and grandparents there were my brothers and sisters and some uncles and aunts – thirteen altogether. We had to sleep on the landing, and then there were the rats, they once found one in bed with me – it was a big one too!

In 1946, we moved out of Greenrow and went to squat in the old RAF huts at West Silloth, next to Stanwix's farm. There were quite a few huts and each one was divided into four family units which opened off a long corridor. We had a living room with a bit of a kitchen in it and two bedrooms. There was a pot-bellied stove which burnt coal.

The washing and toilet facilities were outside.

As you went into the field, there was a Guard House. I don't know what was in there – it was always kept locked. There was an underground Air Raid Shelter, with grass growing on top. My dad had been working on building The Crofts and had a bit of an accident. He got some compensation and went mad with the money. He bought a pig and kept in the Air Raid Shelter! Tommy Cooper from Blitterlees put a ring through its nose. We never ate the pig, Dad sold it over again and bought a two berth caravan with the money!

There was a big emergency reservoir full of water. A little boy drowned in that; I think that even an adult would have had difficulty getting out – the sides were so steep.

We lived there until about 1952, paying five shillings a week rent to the council. Then we all moved into The Crofts

The families used the original coal-burning stoves in the huts for both heating and cooking.

Fatal Rail

Crash

On October 23rd 1950 the 1.15 train from Carlisle to Silloth came off the rails at New Dykes Bridge, half-a-mile east of Kirkbride station. Driver Jackson and Fireman Pearson, both from Carlisle, died when their engine plunged through a fence and buried itself eight feet deep in a boggy field.

All four coaches left the track. Although their wheels were wrenched off and the windows broken, they remained upright. None of the thirty passengers suffered serious injury.

Fire engines and ambulances from Carlisle, Wigton, Silloth and Workington arrived quickly, along with a doctor. The firemen started to cut away the cab in an attempt to free the bodies of the crew but were unable to reach them until heavy lifting gear arrived from the railway depot at Carlisle.

A week later, a Ministry of Transport Inspector held an inquiry into the crash. A fireman, who worked the line regularly, told him that the engine involved, a class J39, was subject to rolling and swaying. "It has never put the wind up me," he said, "but I have known a driver close his regulator and slacken speed because of the swaying."

Other witnesses said that drivers had complained about 'rough riding' on the line. A line patrolman told the inspector that he had walked the line on the morning in question and found no problems. Although there had been heavy rain on the previous day, he did not think it could have had any effect on the track formation at the place where the accident occurred.

At the inquest on the two dead men, the coroner heard evidence that the train was travelling at around 45mph, a normal speed for the stretch of line. In returning a verdict of Accidental Death, he said "Here we have an extraordinary accident; a train on a single line and evidence that there was no obstacle on the track. The line was in good order and there was nothing wrong with the engine." He hoped that the Railway Executive might soon give some indication of the cause of the crash so that the travelling public on the line could be reassured. "As it is," he concluded, "nobody knows what happened."

The final report of the Ministry of Transport inquiry blamed the crash on "a heavy engine being run over light and inadequately maintained track at too high a speed".

Farming Snapshots

The Wilsons lived at Aldoth Farm for many years. It was a mixed farm, growing mostly root vegetables with a small dairy herd. Charles and Mary Wilson handed the farm over to their son, George, and daughter-in-law, Vina, around 1950.

George was a go-ahead sort of fellow and had the first tractor in Aldoth. The little Fordson, with its tyre-less front wheels, was his pride and joy but it was soon replaced with a new Fordson Major.

At Haymaking, and other busy times on the farm, friends and relatives always gave a hand. One regular visitor was Vina Wilson's brother-in-law, Albert Weir. He was a miner who lived in Manchester but loved to visit Aldoth.

George and Vina had three children: George, Harry and Mary.

George instructs his cousin, Ted Wilson, on the mechanical intricacies of his first Fordson.

Albert Weir in charge of the new Fordson Major, 1947.

Charles, looking pleased with the new Ayrshire, 1947.

Friends and relations helping out at haytime. **Left to right:** *Cousin, George Wilson from Haltwhistle; Ike Ross from Silloth; George (obscured); Jackie Johnson, Co-op Insurance man and young Harry.*

George with daughter, Mary, 1954. The curious structure, leaning against the barn wall is one of three galvanised water troughs which George bought. It fed water to the milk cooler inside the farm building. The family think it may originally have had some military function and came from an Army Surplus Auction.

Few farmers were as keen on the new mechanised methods as George Wilson.
At nearby Smart Hill and at Marsh Farm in Skinburness, the Lightfoot and Wannop families still relied on horses.

Harvesting at Smart Hill, 1947.

George Wannop rides Bunty past his home at Marsh Farm while faithful Rap looks on.

Ferreting

Ferreting for rabbits was a popular and often profitable hobby enjoyed by both country people and town dwellers.

The hunters would find a warren where the rabbits had multiple entrances to their burrows. Nets would be placed over some of these and the ferret sent down from another. After a bit of scuttling around underground, the rabbits would start to run out into the nets. They would be caught and their necks pulled.

These pictures show Ian Nattrass and Graham Nelson in action. Ian's brother, John Nattrass, recalls the boys went on regular hunts near Armathwaite, where they lived in the 1940s. They would take the rabbits to a butcher in Warwick Road, Carlisle. This produced some welcome pocket money to buy extra treats during their school lunch breaks.

Listening for action underground

Bottoms Up!

Setting the ferret to work.

Silloth Convalescent Home

This souvenir postcard of the Convalescent Home features Matron H. McCracken who was appointed in 1948, just as the new National Health Service was introduced.

The home had operated as an independent charity ever since it opened in 1862. Most of its patients were sent by the Cumberland Infirmary in Carlisle and it was hoped that, once the NHS took over there, they would operate the home as an annex to the main hospital.

However, it quickly became apparent that this was not to be. It was only in 1951 that an arrangement was made with the NHS to finance some of the patients and, in the meantime, the home struggled on through financial crisis after crisis to provide its services.

Gone Fishin'

Stanley and Cyril Akitt aboard the 'Ann'

The 'Ann' beached for cleaning, about 1935. Note the auxiliary propeller.

Fishing has always been a key part of life for the local people. During the twentieth century, much of this commercial fishing took place at Silloth. A fleet of small vessels was based in the harbour and several local families made their living from seafood. The Baxter, Wilson, Irving and Woodman families all ran boats there.

Then there was the Akitt family. Thomas Akitt came to Silloth from Aspatria in the 1870s and worked at the docks for much of his life. His descendants were also involved with the port and, eventually, in fishing.

Brothers Stanley and Cyril Akitt became fisherman after they left school, in the 1930s. At first they worked for other boat operators such as Dick Woodhouse. After a break caused by the war, during which they both served in the Royal Navy, they bought their own fishing boat, the 'Ann' from Mr Woodhouse; she had an engine but was fully rigged for sail as well.

They fitted a new engine to her themselves and for a while she sported a tubular steel mast which acted as an exhaust pipe and carried the engine fumes up, well away from the deck. They always kept a 'jib sail', stowed in the forecastle, in case of engine failure.

Stan or 'Quag' was a well-known character in Silloth. One of his sayings, after a poor day's catch, was "what a carry on for a scone!"

During the 1950s, the brothers supplemented their income from fishing by offering boat trips to visitors. Fishermen often rose at or before dawn, and only stayed ashore if the weather was really rough. They could leave port at most states of the tide. Fishing was usually done in the hours either side of Low tide. In the summer they fished for shrimps and prawns and, in winter, for skate and plaice. The boats stayed within the Solway, going across to the Scottish side sometimes but never the open sea. The shrimps were washed and sorted as the boat returned. Once in the dock, the catch would be salted and put in boxes before being despatched to fish markets elsewhere. However, some was sold off the boat to holidaymakers in summer.

Stanley Akitt with Jackie Bell holding Louise Todd and a flounder.

Steaming ahead: Stan and young Colin Akitt.

In 1955, Cyril ceased to fish, leaving Stan to carry on with part-time help from other relatives like nephews Jim Bell and Colin Akitt.

Over the years the catches got smaller and less varied. The number of boats decreased as people found other work. By the 1960s, it was not possible to earn a living from fishing.

As well as fishing, the Akitt family were closely involved with the docks. Isaac (1865-1950) worked at the Hydraulic engine house in the early decades of the century. His grandson, Colin, worked for a spell on the cranes and then became a dock-gate man until he retired in 1996; during the 1960s, he also carried out diving tasks for maintenance work.

After he ceased to fish, Colin's brother, Cyril, also worked as a docker and dock-gate man, from 1960 until he retired in the 1980s.

Boat crew working near the dock entrance, around 1960. Colin Akitt in diving gear.

Cyril's son, Colin, worked as a docker and dock-gate man from the 1960s onward. In the 1970s, Cyril, Colin Senr, Colin Junr and George Selkirk, who was a relation, manned the dock-gates. As well as the job of opening the gates, they carried out a variety of work for the port.

Colin Akitt and his cousin, Jim Bell, preparing the boat for sea, 1961.

On the waterfront

Silloth docks in 1947. In the far corner lies the tug 'Petrel', almost at the end of her days.
Ivan Lomas' yacht 'Roamer' which was a converted lifeboat is alongside it.

Immediately after the war the docks at Silloth were still busy handling the diverted coal. In addition, the government set about the rather dubious practice of shipping unwanted military supplies, shells, bombs, out of the port for 'burial' at sea. The operation was run by the Royal Army Service Corps, who used small cargo vessels and other craft to take the old munitions out. Vessels regularly loaded the dangerous cargo between 1947 and 1949.

Dumping the unused ammunition at sea from what were known locally as the 'Bomb Boats'.

However, by 1950, both this and the extra coal traffic had stopped and the port was back to 'normal'. Trade was at a lower level, the only regular traffic now was wheat for the mill. Concerns were voiced about the future of the docks. The 'Assaroe' had stopped calling in 1943 and the trades in slate, wood and coke had all finished.

The docks were arguably saved by Carrs new animal feed mill which led to more grain being shipped in. In addition, Pumice for the British Plaster & Board company and steel ingot moulds going to Holland kept the port active, though not busy, through these years.

In 1948, 'Petrel', the paddle-tug which had worked out of Silloth for more than 50 years, made her final journey – to Corpach on Loch Linnhe in Scotland where she was dismantled.

With its old buildings and equipment, surrounded by a network of rusting rail tracks, the port took on a rather disused and neglected appearance.

Two familiar faces at the port in these years were the Stronach Brothers. Arthur and Stuart Stronach ran the shipbroking and agency business which was set up by their grandfather in the 1860s. The office was on Station road. Arthur lived on Skinburness road, Stuart in Blitterlees. They retired and sold the business in 1968.

J. Arthur Stronach, DFC, MBE, JP.
Arthur served in the Royal Flying Corps
during the First World War.

PORT MARKS

All fishing vessels at Silloth carry the letters CL. This actually stands for Carlisle – because Silloth is on the stretch of coast (Ellenfoot to Sarkfoot) which was historically designated as the port of Carlisle. The Government has not yet recognised Silloth as a port of registry.

J. D. Stuart Stronach

Some Happy Campers

Two Carlisle families who visited Silloth regularly were the Wrights and the Stirlings. The Wrights had their own chalet on Stanwix's field; the Stirlings just hired a caravan for the week. Here they are enjoying some of the attractions at Silloth in the post-war years........

The Wrights picnic down by the old battery house, Blitterlees.

Below: *The ladies take to the water! In the late 1940s.*

Below: *On the roundabout.*

Parked up and picnicking somewhere on the banks around 1950

The Stirling family at West Beach and with the ponies. Mid 50s.

. . . and round the town

Left: *Locals taking a trip with 'Pop' Carr.*

Peter Ostle from Aspatria takes a ride. 1946.

Left: *Youthful bathing beauties!*

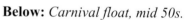

Below: *Carnival float, mid 50s.*

22MU

After the war, the RAF airfield at Silloth became purely a maintenance unit. Their main work was stripping the equipment from redundant aircraft and sending the fuselage on to the High Duty Alloys factory, near Workington, where it was re-cycled.

The civilian workforce was headed by a small contingent of RAF Personnel. In the late 1950s, the airfield also became the headquarters of Cumberland Aviation Services Ltd. This company hired out light aircraft for charter flights, executive travel and crop spraying. For a few years, around that time, there were also scheduled flights to the Isle of Man from Silloth. These were operated, first, by Manx Airways and later by Silver City Airways. The forerunner of Silver City, British Aviation Services, had become involved with Silloth in 1946. They ferried war surplus aircraft all over the world, mostly Douglas DC3 Dakotas which were stored at 22MU. These were refurbished in Canada and then delivered to European airlines for use on commercial routes.

Douglas Dakotas and an Avro Yorks bomber, in storage for future scrapping at Silloth during the early 1950s.

Auster Workmaster

Boarding a de Havilland Rapide for a flight to the Isle of Man in 1958, en route to the TT races. Local jet-setter, Lawrence Marshall, second from right.

22MU Photo Album

The station's fire crew, 1955.

(Left To Right) Back Row:- Firemen: Jacky Wilson, Tom Wood, Senior Fireman Geoff Watson, Firemen: Paddy Loughlin and Fred Armstrong.

Front Row:- Fireman Frank Linton, Head Fireman Harry Gibbons, W/Com. Booth.(C.O.), Fire Officer Killon. Fireman George Potts.

A formal group of RAF and civilian personnel pose in front of a Twin Pioneer, 1959.

Jackie Tinnion at work in the radio shops.

Some of the 'Civvies'.

Back Row (l to r): Bill Bouch (Lab.), Fred Crombie, Ernie Logan, George Sewell, John Cowan, Joe Briggs (All Radio Technicians).

Front Row: (l to r) Bunny Selkirk (Motor Transport), John Lowes, Bob Gibson. Unknown Visitor, Ron Barker, Pat Barton (Radio Technicians).

Bob Gibson remembers . . .

After the war, I stayed on working on the airfield in the radio workshops at the Maintenance Unit there. They kept on eight radio technicians to work on the CADF (Commutated Antenna Direction Finding) Equipment.

If an aircraft got into trouble it would send out a signal on the 243 Mc/s emergency frequency. This would be picked-up by our equipment. When this happened, radar screens at London and Prestwick Airports would show a line, shooting out from Silloth in the direction of the signal. Other stations would also pick up the signal and they would see where the lines crossed – that would indicate the position of the aircraft. This was transferred to the big maps in London and they could see exactly where it was.

As the pilot flew north or south, we might loose the signal but other stations would pick it up so they could keep track of the plane. I think the same system was used all over Europe.

The Silloth MU closed in December 1960 but I, along with seven other technicians, remained at Silloth to man the CADF equipment, night and day, on a shift system. Eventually we were moved to 14MU at Carlisle. I carried on working there until 1985 when I retired.

The CADF equipment then went automatic and digital – called Digital Reference Direction Finding and, as far as I know, continued operating for many years.

The Digital Reference Direction finding Equipment at Silloth.

Right and above right:

The Radio Workshop at 22MU during the 1950s.

A Seaside Theatre

Silloth Pavilion in pre-war days; among the acts billed are the 'Zeal Players'.

Since Edwardian times, an area of Silloth Green, known as the Happy Valley, had been home to various troupes of seaside entertainers. In 1929, the district council leased the area and turned it into an indoor theatre: The Pavilion.

Enclosing the former Pierrot stage and the hill behind, the wooden building contained a stage, an auditorium with 600 tip seats plus dressing rooms for the performers. Over the next twenty years, it became the venue for many entertainments, notably Charles Beanland's Silloth Follies who performed there throughout the summer between 1934 and 1939. During the winter, the Silloth Choral and Dramatic Societies put on shows there.

Normal summer shows resumed after the war. The building was let to tenants, usually on an annual basis, and, at first, various touring parties from around the UK performed.

Then, in 1950, work began on the new sea wall. During this time Costains, the main contractor, used the building as their canteen and rest rooms. It seems they knocked the place about a bit and, rather than pay for repairs, they bought the building from the local council.

A group of amateur pierrots from Carlisle who performed in the Pavilion some time before its closure.

PAVILION, SILLOTH
The Finest Concert Hall on the Cumberland Coast

OFFICIAL OPENING

MONDAY, JUNE 24TH AT 8.30 P.M.

Under the Patronage and presence of Members of the HOLME CULTRAM URBAN DISTRICT COUNCIL.

THE REVUSICAL CABERET TAB SHOW
"COMPLIMENTS"
Will Appear
DAILY AT 3.00 at 8.30 p.m. during the week.
BOOK YOUR SEATS FOR THIS BIG EVENT
ADMISSION – 1/3, 1/- AND 6d.
(Including Tax)

All the leading Concert Party Attractions have been secured for the Silloth Season.

Don't miss visiting the Silloth Pavilion – The Concert Hall de-luxe.

Organised Outings, School Parties, Scouts, Guides and similar organisations quoted special rates on application to the Entertainments Manager.

Press advertisement for the opening show in 1929.

Gus Proud remembers . . .

My father worked in the old Pavilion when he was a youngster – he was the chocolate boy and used to go round in the interval selling his wares. He had aspirations of being on the stage; he never made it but I did!

During the war, they had Saturday afternoon talent shows for the kids. There were tables on stage, full of chocolates and sweets for prizes. These things were all rationed – I don't know where they got hold of such quantities. I performed 'Under the Spreading Chestnut Tree' with all the actions and I won a box of chocolates.

The Pavilion was a marvellous place. It was a wooden-framed building with tongue and grove boards nailed on to the outside. The rear was built over the hill which formed a natural embankment and the seats were tiered up that. It was quite cosy inside. There could be a gale howling outside but it was nice and warm in there.
When we were lads, we couldn't afford to go to the shows so we chiselled out a spy-hole in the back wall and watched them through that! They used to block it up with putty, but we just opened it up again.

Once, a rumour spread round the school that a fan-dancer was going to appear. We went to the Saturday afternoon show to see her. She danced around with these huge ostrich feathers and then, right at the end of her act, she spread out her arms to reveal all – and then they turned off the lights. When they came on again, she had vanished. That was my first glimpse of a naked women but it wasn't much of a view!

The shows changed every week. There were singers and dancers and conjurers. They continued putting on good shows during the war. The lads on the aerodrome formed a band, The Silloth Modernairs, it was brilliant. Fred Irons was the band leader - he played violin and clarinet. Paddy Burns was a marvellous singer with a superb tenor voice. Shirley Sim, a lovely soprano, also sang in the band.

After the war, the local Amateur Dramatics Society did plays there. About 1948, they put on a play in which my then girlfriend, Margaret Robinson, played a policewoman. I thought she was going to end up a star, but obviously there were no talent spotters at the show.

In 1950, I started to serve my time with Tommy Underwood as a joiner. One of my first jobs was dismantling the pavilion. We took the boards off the outside, knocked out the nails, and transported most of them to Stanwix's caravan site where we built six holiday chalets from the remains. They were close to the old Hospital Bungalow, where Miss Dodds lived in those days. She used to bring our Ten O'Clocks out for us. As well as the boss, Tom Underwood, and his son Tom, there was Alan Riddick, Tom Wilson, and me working there. I'm the only one of them still around.

Three of the chalets which Gus and the team built from the remains of the pavilion were still standing and still in use at the end of the century. The owners had covered the outside walls with flat asbestos sheeting.

CHAPTER EIGHT
The Sixties and Seventies

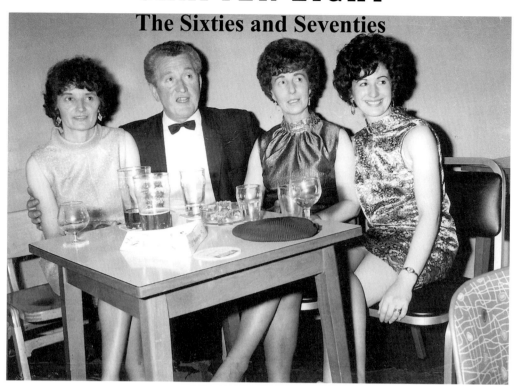

Doris Wilson, Bill, Margaret and Carolyn Richardson. Carrs' Christmas Social at the Cosmo Ballroom, Carlisle, 1967.

During the early sixties, several events occurred which had a lasting effect on the economy of the local area. The Ministry of Defence sold off the wartime airfield at Silloth and the railway line from the town to Carlisle closed. Following the election of a Labour government in 1964, the whole of West Cumberland became a 'Special Development Area'. Generous grants were available to firms who re-located or expanded there – the more people they employed, the more money they got.

Several men, some local and some from further afield, saw the business opportunities which these changes presented. Over the next few years, the sleepy Solway Plain finally caught up with the rest of the country and, in places, even began to swing a little.

The airfield became the site for the Lido, other tourist attractions and home to several new businesses. The end of the cheap railway day trips forced other businessmen to seek different customers and soon a new breed of visitor began to flood into the area. New holiday camps and caravan sites opened, not only in Silloth but all along the coast. Most of these new visitors came in their own cars. Local people also became far more mobile. Cars were now affordable. People developed a taste for new forms of entertainment and culture.

After 1973, when Britain joined the European Community, further grants became available to business from Brussels. Local farmers also benefitted from the community's Common Agricultural Policy which guaranteed them a fair price for absolutely anything they chose to produce.

Agriculture became more mechanised and far fewer men were needed for work on the land. Tourism, light industry and road transport became equally important employers and attracted new workers to the area. Many came from the still depressed mining areas in West Cumberland.

By the end of the seventies, the Solway Plain changed radically. It was now attracting not only large numbers of holiday makers but also many new residents. It had become a popular place to live, especially for retired people – a trend which was to continue right to the end of the century.

New Industries

In 1960, the RAF vacated Silloth Aerodrome. The huge complex now lay empty, but was considered a site with great potential.

Auctioneers Harrison & Hetherington were appointed to sell the land, which was divided into lots. The first auction was held in September 1962 but there was little interest at first. Most of the lots did not reach the reserve price and were withdrawn. The majority of buyers were farmers reclaiming land lost when the Air Ministry requisitioned it back in 1938. Indeed there was a special arrangement whereby land would be returned to previous holders if it failed to reach its price.

There were exceptions. Carlisle based Border Developments purchased a large site for a holiday camp and property developers, F. R. Evans of Leeds, bought the main built-up portion.

Further auctions brought limited success but, gradually, with advertising in the national press and the introduction of Government Grants for occupants, local, national, and even international businesses were attracted to Silloth.

Almost all the raw materials and finished goods were transported by road, greatly increasing the amount of local traffic. The only firm to make use of Silloth docks was Coulthards. Some buildings on the airfield were used as warehouses by road transport companies. These included Carr's Agriculture, and several local hauliers including Pat Hornsby, who carried and stored material for Fisons, and D.A. Harrison whose business was to diversify considerably over the years.

The airfield auction. We believe the two men with glasses, sitting on the front row, are the Evans brothers of Leeds who purchased a large part of the property.

The Firms that came to Silloth

Coulthard's Concrete Products was the first business to arrive. It was formed by two local men: Ernest Thomson, a builder, and Arthur Coulthard, who made concrete building components at Bothel, near Cockermouth. They purchased two hangars plus some land at Blackdyke and began making various products for the building industry.

The operation grew and, in 1969, the firm patented a special lightweight breezeblock made using pumice. The volcanic pumice was imported from Lipari in the Mediterranean, through Silloth docks.

Carnation made children's art materials such as crayons and blackboards. Its two partners relocated their factory from the London area in 1968. They employed up to 100 people and the general manager, David Pigeon, became a Mayor of Silloth.

Kurt Oppenheim established **The Cumberland Curled Hair Co.** at Whitehaven in 1945. It originally produced filling for beds and furnishings using curled and treated animal hair; a process which his family had been using since the early nineteenth century. In 1964, he purchased land and two hangars next to the main road at Causewayhead and moved manufacturing there.
Animal hair was brought to the site and washed, treated, given a curl, and then dried. The processed hair was sold to manufacturers of furniture and upholstery, to fill the cushions in their products.

The same firm developed another product in 1960 **Cheri-Foam** - a new, synthetic filling for cushions. This was a patent polyurethane foam,

made by a 'secret' chemical process. It became very popular with seating manufacturers.

A variation, with different properties, was also developed called 'Cheri-Tex'. Both materials came out of the production process as long rectangular blocks before being cut to whatever size the customer desired.

Both hair and foam operations were successful. 60 people were employed in 1966 and over 100 by the mid-1970s.

Micaply was a Californian Company which set up their plant in 1969 inside one of the large hangars. They produced glass epoxy laminates which were used to make printed circuit boards and insulating components in electronic equipment. The operation employed 150 by the late 1970s and maintained strong links with . . .

Printing Techniques Ltd / Yates. This British based (but American-owned) company manufactured the copper foil used by the electronics industry in printed circuit boards. It was made through electrolysis, where electrodes placed in a copper solution form solid copper. The equipment produced a continuous sheet of foil which was wound onto drums. The company set up their plant in one of the former RAF buildings and later expanded to occupy a large Hangar.

In 1964, the Ardmore Steel Company expressed an interest in using the outer dock at silloth for breaking up old ships and salvaging the resulting steel. Despite the closure of the railway, which nearly stopped the plan, the company went ahead and the first ships arrived the following year. A total of ten vessels were dismantled, including two ex-Royal Navy minesweepers. Some of the old metalwork was exported directly to Germany.

Established at Hexham, Northumberland, in 1932, the Tynedale Auction Company also took an interest in Silloth dock. This cattle trading business was looking for a suitable place where

The Micaply Factory.

they could build a lairage to rest and feed cows after their sea voyage from Ireland.

They erected a large building with an office alongside the inner dock. It was built on the site of an older lairage used when the 'Assaroe' brought animals to from Dublin. The long Victorian transit shed which had dominated the south side of the inner dock was dismantled. Fred Peart, minister for agriculture, opened the new facility in July 1968.

The livestock was usually shipped from Greenore by Franz Buitelaar Ltd of Boston in Lincolnshire. At first, the cattle were taken by road to Hexham for sale but, after a few years, Tynedale chose to sell and distribute the animals to other marts directly from Silloth. The operation of the lairage was overseen by Wallace Bissett.

Shipbreaking operations in the outer or Marshall dock, 1967.

(Right) *The Lairage.*

The end of the line

The last train to Silloth ran on Sunday, September 7th 1964. Fifty years later, people were still claiming that this event marked the 'death of Silloth'. In fact, in a perverse way, the closure of the rail line may have marked the start of the town's resurrection rather than its death.

In March 1963, Dr Richard Beeching had published his report 'The Reshaping of British Railways'. It proposed that 6,000 miles of track should be closed in order to save the vast amounts of tax-payers' money being used to subsidise rural branch lines. The Carlisle to Silloth line was one of those facing the axe.

A public hearing by the Transport Users' Consultative Committee was held at Carlisle on October 2nd 1963. A petition from Silloth Parish Council, signed by 8,000 people was handed in.

British Railways reported that total receipts from the line were £16,900 per year - £46 a day. It was losing £27,000 per year (around a quarter-of-a-million at 2011 prices) and needed investment of a further £31,570 in the near future.

A census of passengers had been taken over a representative period in 1963. This showed a daily average of 264 getting on and off the trains at Silloth. The daily average at Abbeytown was 10, at Blackdyke it was 5. On Sundays during the summer period the number of passengers joining and alighting at Silloth varied between one and 800. A far cry from the thousands who had travelled on bank holiday weekends between the wars.

The BR spokesman said on the preceding Tuesday, 89 paying passengers travelled on the line. 38 people booked at Carlisle and 51 used the line to travel from Silloth to Carlisle. All the figures showed the numbers were steadily decreasing. The number of passengers using the intermediate stations on a regular basis seldom reached double figures.

Another important factor in the decision to close the line, although not mentioned at the hearing in Carlisle, must have been the complete collapse of freight traffic. By 1963, Carrs' Flour Mill was exclusively using road transport. Fisons had ceased manufacturing operations at Silloth but had retained the site as a distribution centre which also used road transport. The only firm importing through the docks and still using the rail link was Andersons, the timber merchants of Carlisle. The Beeching report listed Silloth as generating less than 5,000 tons of freight per year; this wouldn't amount to more than one or two wagons a day.

At the hearing in Carlisle, the objectors to closure of the line were required to produce evidence that it would produce 'hardship' for local people; this they singularly failed to do. The only group of people who would be inconvenienced

A Diesel Multiple Unit arrives at a virtually deserted Silloth station in the early 60s. The line had been among the first in the country to use these trains.

One man who lost his job as a result of the rail closure was Joe Wise, the gate-keeper at Causewayhead level crossing.

were students attending college in Carlisle who would not be able to get there by bus for 9am. The only local business to be seriously affected was Ivan Lomas, the fishmonger, who would now have to collect his supplies from Aspatria station.

The representatives of the local councils made long and impassioned speeches to the committee but were unable to produce a single example of anybody using the line to travel to work. Based on the overwhelming economic arguments for closure, the Committee overruled the objectors and fixed the date on which Dr Beeching's plans would be implemented.

On the last day of services, there were dramatic scenes at Silloth station. A steam-hauled train replaced the usual diesel railcar. Protesters laid down on the tracks in front of it. A wreath was fixed on the front of the engine. There were people all along the line to Carlisle waving goodbye.

Silloth's rail link entered the realms of local folklore and the rose-tinted memories of rail enthusiasts; the local people got on perfectly well without it. A year after the closure, during the July Carlisle Race Week, the Carlisle Journal interviewed some of them. B.T.Garrett, manager of the Queens Hotel, told them he had seen no drop in his trade at all. "So far I am up eighty guests over last year, but bar trade is slightly down, I have noticed a lot more cars in town", he said. Malcolm Wilson of the Silloth Motor Company agreed that there were just as many people staying in the hotels and said that he had heard almost all the caravan sites were full up. Another local told the reporter "I have noticed a lot more cars here but the West Beach seems to be deserted; it was never like that before."

Perhaps the new breed of holiday-makers, who had arrived in their own cars, had discovered that, not just Silloth, but the whole of the Solway Plain was an ideal centre for touring. Less than an hour's drive away there was the most beautiful landscape in England, the historic places of interest in Carlisle and along Hadrian's Wall plus Gretna and the Scottish lowlands just a little further on. They discovered all of this plus the miles of perfect sandy beaches along toward Allonby which now, even on Bank Holidays, were never over-crowded.

THE LAST TRAIN FROM SILLOTH

"We'd better hurry Doc—or we'll miss the last train!"

The Carlisle Journal cartoonist's take on the closure.
Willie Whitelaw was the local M.P.

Silloth station is emptied of its furniture following the closure.

The BPA

The two pictures above and many others featured in this chapter, come from the Border Press Agency which was run by John and Peter Barker in Carlisle.

Between 1957 and 1977, they and a small staff supplied local news and photos to a variety of national publications. They also produced their own such as the long-running *'Lakescene'* magazine.

Their records were deposited with Cumbria Archives Service and, thanks to them, and to John Barker, we have been able to use some excellent snapshots of life in these years including this fabulous portrait of William Hurst. Mr Hurst made news in October 1969, when he reached one hundred years of age.

He farmed at Pelutho for many years and, later, near Penrith. He spent his last years with his son, Joseph, and daughter-in-law, Mary Ann, on Skinburness road. On his birthday, he was given a special party and gifts by the Solway Over-60s club at The Towers.

When the new dock gates were installed at Silloth, in 1967, he recalled seeing the first ones being put on in 1885. William went on to live another three years, passing away in 1972.

Airfield sport and leisure

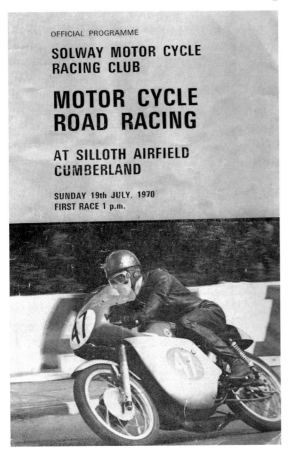

Motorcycle road racing

Jack Horseman brought Motorbike racing to Silloth in 1964. He lived at Dalston near Carlisle and was a former racing champion at national level. He had wanted to bring the sport to Cumberland for several years. His dream was realised when permission was granted for such events on the ex-RAF Airfield at Silloth.

The first racing was held on a Sunday in July 1964. It attracted many top riders from all over Britain. A five hour programme was arranged for that first day, comprising five solo and two side-car races. Admission was free and the track occupied an area at the Northern end of the aerodrome, on land belonging to Mr. Holliday. This first event was staged by the North East Motorcycle Racing Club.

Around 10,000 people turned up to watch the races on that first day. 110 riders from as far away as Dundee, Gateshead, Sheffield, Barnsley and Preston

showed off their skill. Top overall performer was National champion George Buchan of Inverness.

After that first meeting, races were held regularly for the next twelve years. Meetings were held between May and September by the Solway Motorcycle Racing Club, which was formed shortly after the first meeting. This club was affiliated to the National association. Racing was split into different classes according to engine size and number of wheels – 3-wheel and sidecar events were included.

On two occasions the circuit hosted the National Championships. High profile riders from all over the U.K. came to Silloth but very few Cumbrians took part. However, some locals helped out at the course, including Lawrence Marshall, who provided commentary during the races for several years.

The races attracted large audiences from well beyond the Solway Plain.

Hell Drivers!

A few years later, another form of motor racing arrived on the Airfield - The Hell Drivers.

Stock car racing, or helldriving, came to this country from America. It was growing in popularity but had not been seen in Northwest England until it arrived at Silloth.

The sport was brought there by Leeds businessman Jeff Brownhut, who got permission to hold the events on the airfield early in 1972.

Jeff and business partner Ian Thomas had brought Speedway motorcycle races to Derwent Park at Workington. It was intended to set up regular stock car racing there too but the track proved unsuitable. They became aware of a possible site at Silloth through someone he knew at the property developers F R Evans & Co, who were based in Leeds (Like Jeff) and now controlled the commercial land at the airfield. An arrangement was made for Jeff and Ian to create a track and facilities.

He also ran stock car racing at other towns including Peterborough, in partnership with Geoff Penniket

SILLOTH RACEWAY
Silloth
Cumberland

OFFICIAL
12p
MAGAZINE
PROGRAMME

HELL DRIVERS

Sunday 29th April 1973 at 3.0 p.m.

LLOYD BRO'S TROPHY
PLUS
"THE ALL GIRL" POWDER PUFF
plus THE VERY FIRST RAMP RACE
"THE GRAND NATIONAL"
2nd Season 2nd Meeting.

and in the North East with Mike Parker. They were joined by Ron Cooper for the Silloth events.

A test race was made by four of the country's top drivers in the Helldrivers Association, which at the time had 880 members. Following this, the first official meeting was fixed for Easter that year.

Transit rescue van

At first drivers were brought from Newcastle until there were enough trained drivers in Cumbria. As more local men approached Jeff with the hope of competing, a pool of drivers was built up and a league was set up. The local lads were joined by men from all over the North of England & Scotland as the sport caught on.

Jeff Brownhut formed Cumbrian Raceways, which hosted the Silloth meetings in the years that followed.

The weekly race meetings were made into public –friendly events with more than just car racing. Refreshments and side shows were put on so that families could enjoy a day out. Crowds came down to watch the dramatic sport, where the roar of engines and smell of burning rubber accompanied the speed, danger – and crashes!

Unlike the motorbike races, most of the drivers were Cumbrian. Among the people who took part were: Brian 'Lofty' Stoddart, Eric Davenport, Dave Joyce, Willy Morgan, Bob Pattinson, Eddy Bosward, and Danny Baxter. These men enjoyed scouring local scrapyards and garages for suitable cars, modifying and personalising them, so they could perform well in – and survive – the rough sport.

Included in some of the meetings were all-women events known as the 'Powder Puff Derby'. These were open to girlfriends and family of the drivers.

The men (left to right) Lofty Stoddart, John Stamper, Bobby Charters and Gordon Jamieson. We think the girls must have been supplied by the race sponsors – Player's No 6 !

139

The Northwest Shows

Out of the Hell Drivers was born what could be regarded as the greatest outdoor attractions ever held on the Solway Plain – The Northwest Shows. According to the Cumberland News, it was an army careers advisor, manning a display at one of the Race meetings in 1973, who suggested to Jeff Brownhut "you could make this into a big event".

Inspired and excited by the idea, he set about contacting people and groups who could perform, exhibit or entertain and make the event a real attraction. In just a few months, he managed to put together an impressive programme.

The result was the first North West Show, which was held on Silloth Airfield over two days on August bank holiday 1973.

The show consisted of a programme of stock car racing, around which was provided a host of entertainments for all the family.

A 'Miss Northwest' contest was held, with entrants from a wide area. The Eagles free-fall parachute display team performed for the crowd, as did John Penny 'The Red Baron' in a replica of an early Fokker aircraft he had built himself.

Crowds watched the 'Motorcycle Madmen' stunt team perform dangerous feats, including riding through blazing hoops – and attempt to set a new world record. This was for the longest ride through fire, then set at sixty feet. Rider Dave Ousby of Penrith took up the challenge and rode for seventy-two feet through the blazing hoops.

Other features included a large motor show with cars supplied by local dealers, a display of army vehicles and equipment, marching bands and a wide selection of sales stands, displays and refreshment booths. Lined up, the whole event represented six miles of attractions.

SILLOTH RACEWAY, SILLOTH-ON-SOLWAY, CUMBERLAND.

NORTHWEST 73

26/27 AUGUST 1973.

OFFICIAL MAGAZINE PROGRAMME

Stock Car racing was still the main attraction.

Central to all was the stock car action. A number of different races, staged within each day's meeting, were sponsored by various local and national enterprises. Over forty drivers entered. The first day's driving awards were presented by Jackie Charlton, manager of Middlesbrough Football Club, who was ferried to Silloth in a white Rolls Royce courtesy of Peter Connon.

Drivers who picked up awards included Harry Parker of Penrith, John Stamper of Wigton, Andy Ostle and Ivan Leeson, both from Aspatria. Drivers from the North-east also took part.

In the 'Powder Puff Derby' first prize was taken by Linda Pearson of Silloth, her third win. Like other races at the time, this event was sponsored by a well-known brand of cigarette, in this case 'Players No. 10'.

The event was a phenomenal success. Press reports state that over 30,000 people turned up in total over the two days, causing, at one point, a queue of traffic several miles long on the main B5302 road to Silloth.

Even as the first event was being held, grand plans for Northwest '74 were being drawn up.

Carolyn Richardson makes a parachute landing at the Armed Forces Display.

Eric Davenport remembers. . .

The Hell Drivers was a big thing back then. We used to get huge crowds, there was a big following from locals and from further away too. It was a great time. Cars were cheap to buy, you could pick up one from a scrapyard for £5. Fuel was cheap.

We competed in the North of England League. Sometimes we went to other venues such as Motherwell in Scotland or Newton Aycliffe in Durham. We went in Pop Carr's bus, somehow we got the cars there as well. The top course was the White City track in Manchester. I got as far as the national finals and was leading for much of the final race, but then I lost power. Afterwards I discovered why, a piece of sawdust had found its way into the fuel pipe. You had to make sure your car was strong enough to last the race. Speed wasn't as important as strength on the Silloth track. We fitted steel bars and reinforced the cars. Concrete was even used - whatever worked. Local garages were kept busy making vehicles as durable and slick as possible.

Pop Carr's bus.

Later Events

NorthWest '74 was held on the May bank Holiday and had the same format – car racing plus a range of other activities.

Thousands poured in to see famous escapologist 'The Great Crossini' at work, stunt driver Jon Marshall's driving feats, a Japanese martial art display team, the Blue Eagles Air Display Corps, and helicopter flights. On display were a variety of cars old and new, military vehicles, hovercraft, police, fire and rescue vehicles as well as the usual stalls and refreshment stands.

The stock car circuit was central to all this. Action took place throughout the weekend but, this year, a large truck trailer was parked in the centre. On this, as well as local music groups, celebrities Norman Collier and Ken Dodd appeared along with actors from popular television shows. Border Television presenter, Derek Batey, staged his popular 'Mr and Mrs' show and acted as public announcer. Like the first, it was a huge success drawing many thousands.

THE
CUMBRIA EXHIBITION
AND THE
ESSO UNIFLO CUMBRIA RUN

Spring Bank Holiday
25th & 26th May, 1975

SILLOTH RACEWAY
SILLOTH-ON-SOLWAY   CUMBRIA

It was followed in May 1975 by a vintage rally arranged by Jeff and his team. A large number of old vehicles, carefully preserved by their owners, took part in a run from Penrith via Carlisle and Wigton. At Silloth, these formed part of a two-day show also featuring hang-gliding, jet copters, live music and plenty of Hell Driving (using the usual cars, not the classic ones!).

Sponsored by Esso, this 'Cumbria Run and Exhibition' was another ambitious event involving many different organisations.

But, despite the huge success of these ambitious events, it wasn't to last. Several factors brought the races to an end. One was the shortage of old cars. As Hell Driving caught on, the scrapyards and other sources of suitable vehicles began to dry up. It became harder to find one and the price went up as demand grew.

Another issue was the weather. Wet days meant small crowds and smaller takings on the gate which, in turn, meant losses or low profits for the organisers.

A further factor was the amount the drivers were receiving for their work. Anyone who entered a race, with a car they had bought and prepared themselves, got £1. The most anyone could win in prize money was £10 – the award for the overall winner that day; coming second earned £8 and third £6. Winners of each heat got £5. Everyone else received nothing.

The cost of maintaining a car was often well above the income given for performing, and drivers didn't like this position. They got together and asked the organisers to increase the amount to £5 for entering. When this appeal failed, many withdrew. Like the other motor racing on the airfield, the Northwest shows ceased, but very similar events were held instead by the Management of the Lido holiday park, in the 1980s.

You can read about these in the next chapter.

Civil Defence Exercise & Tournament

The Airfield was the setting for the eighth annual Civil Defence Association rally and exercise; held on a Sunday in May 1962, about 3,300 people took part. The aim was to practice skills and tasks necessary in major disaster situations. It was also a tournament with prizes for the best teams. These came from all over the North of England and engaged in such tasks as:

Emergency feeding
Rescuing from buildings
Signalling
Cable laying
Care of homeless
Medical aid
Despatch riding

Each team completed exercises in all of these areas. They were joined by a large number of others who took on the role of people in need – hungry, injured, etc. Various mock disaster situations were enacted so that the teams' training could be put to the test. The Cumberland Team came first in the emergency feeding exercise. This involved preparing and cooking food for 200 people in temporary 'Field Kitchens' and then taking it to them. For this, the members created a meal of steak, creamed potatoes, carrots and beans and a dessert of apples and custard. This was ferried to one of the large hangars where hundreds sat at trestle tables waiting for the food. Cumberland also did well in the rescue and first aid sections.

The event was attended by many MPs and figures in civic affairs, including the chairman of County Council, Tim Westoll. The event was overseen by Regional Civil Defence director, Major S. Lamplugh.

The scale of the rally made it a great spectacle and organisers agreed the airfield was a perfect venue for hosting such events.

The 'casualties' line up for attention.

Farmers in the news

By the 1960s, most farms were becoming highly mechanised but not all embraced the modern methods. Even in the 70s, Vivian Shadwick continued to rely on three Clydesdale horses for the work on Kelsick House Farm near Abbeytown.

Here we see farmhand, John Smith, cutting a crop of oats on a harvester which could have been seen in Victorian times. It wasn't until Vivian retired, around 1980, that his relatives began using tractors on the farm.

The third picture shows some lambs which caused a stir among the farming world in 1962.

Alex, Agnes and William Ramsey Dunlop were the tenants of Stone House Farm at Seaville where they kept around seventy Greyface ewes. Some of these, having birthed a good number of lambs in the Spring, produced a second brood in August-September, something unknown for the breed at the time. It had been attempted before, without success, but the Dunlops managed it without even trying!

Abnormal load

In April 1966, a large piece of industrial plant was taken down the coast road having been brought by ship to Silloth from Manchester. It was going to the new Thames Board Mill near Workington. Heavy Lift contractor Wynns of Newport had the job of hauling it through the coastal villages. Other traffic was, naturally, all but halted!

Passing Allonby's central garage and the riding school.

The load going through the south end of Blitterlees.

The load makes it over the bridge at Allonby.

Entertainments

On Spring Bank Holiday weekend, 1976, a huge choice of entertainment was on offer locally.

At the Holm Cultram Festival in Abbeytown, you could choose between Monty Sunshine and His Jazz Band (£1.50) or the high culture of Leon Gossens and the Fitzwilliam Quartet (75p to £1.50).

The Skinburness Hotel offered dancing to the Trident Sound (50p with late bar) while The Golf also had dancing to the Duhalli Trio on Saturday. On Sunday, the Milvane Trio headlined a Country and Western and Cabaret Night there while, on Monday, there was more dancing with Dave Storey and Reunion. For this event, a collar and tie was to be worn! There was a "Disco as usual in the Cellar Bar". The Queens Hotel had dancing on Saturday only to the Ray Sewell Trio

A little further afield, the Solway Hotel at Allonby had a "Pops Night" with the Brooklyn Sound and, at the White Heather in Kirkbride, there was a choice – Copper Canyon on Friday or Special Bru on Saturday.

The era of 'Swinging Silloth' and begun a few years earlier . . .

Pop Idols

Pattern People aka Paper Sun.

Rue and the Rockets.

The VIPs.

The Meteors from Maryport.

Some of the local groups who performed all around the area in the 60s and 70s.
Rue was a member of the Slater family who ran the amusement side of things at the Lido.

He was still touring with The Rockets at the end of the century!
Greg Ridley, from Aspatria, (second from left in the VIPs) went on to perform as a member of Spooky Tooth and Humble Pie.

The Elite Club

Silloth truly began to swing in early '62, when 71-year-old James Chatham Allen arrived there from London. He leased the run-down Central Hall which, at the time, consisted of a ballroom and billiard hall with a small café upstairs.

Within a few weeks, The Carlisle Journal was hailing him as 'Mr. Silloth' and telling its readers that the Central Hall had been transformed into "what must be the most luxurious club of its type in the North of England". 'J.C.' told the reporter "There's nothing fair-ground style about the Elite Club. It will cater for a variety of tastes in a dignified manner. I feel sure it will go".

Go it did, and so did James Chatham Allen, just a few months later!

Work on the new club was completed very quickly. Several local businessmen were involved. Bob Edgar was the main contractor, Pat Scott supplied the carpets, Joe Abbot and Gus Proud did the joinery. On the opening night, Derek Batey of Border Television introduced Rodney Ware, Carlisle's answer to Frankie Vaughan, along with the Pat Allan Dancers. Johnnie Duncan and the Bluegrass Boys and Russ Abbot were among the artists who appeared in following months.

The club was an immediate success, attracting custom from all parts of the county. As well as the acts on stage, it offered its members the opportunity for a bit of a flutter. There was a roulette wheel and poker schools frequently ran on until 4am.

Then, as suddenly as he had appeared, J.C. Allen vanished, leaving a trail of debts and a number of very angry local tradesmen. These local men took over the club and ran it quite successfully for another five years or so. One of them, Gus Proud, remembers that the committee were not as conscientious as they might have been when it came to meeting the strict legal requirements for a private members club. Guests were not always signed-in, and members' cards were seldom checked. He was on the door one Sunday evening, when twenty-seven policemen raided the place! It seems the management got away with a caution and nobody went to jail.

After the club closed in the early 1970s, the Royal British Legion took over the premises and Silloth never did become the Las Vegas of the north.

*The Elite Club in its heyday
and* **(above)**
in later years.

Barry Hope remembers . . .

In 1972, I was managing the White Heather Club at Kirkbride. One really wet day, I was driving through Silloth and I saw this big new building going up on Stanwix Park at Greenrow. I thought I'd call in and see what was going on.

I walked in and met Eric and Roland 'Dinky' Stanwix working away there. It was utterly miserable inside, the rain was coming through the roof, and it was very dark because it didn't have many windows. We got talking and eventually Eric said "Do you want a job?" and I said "Yes, if the money's right."

So I ended up there. You could basically say that we built it with our bare hands. I did the electrical work, Eric did the steel work and Roland did all sorts of jobs round the site, driving tractors and that sort of thing. It opened on April Fools' Day, 1973, after I'd been there for about a year.

The White Heather had been very much based on entertainment in those days and I carried this on down at Silloth. Sunday was the main pop night and we put on a lot of big names in the Sunset Inn. We had The Bachelors, The Tremolos, The Swinging Blue Jeans, Dave Berry and the Cruisers and Alvin Stardust, who was then performing as Shane Fenton and the Fentones. We had them all after they appeared on Top of The Pops.

It was really just open in the summer but we did open at week-ends in the winter. Our audience came from all over. There were a lot of coaches coming in; not organised by us – they just arrived. Business was boosted in the summer season when we did kids' shows too.

There wasn't a great deal else on the site in those days. There was a play area with swings and roundabouts and the Cyclo-Mobiles were a big draw. They carried three people; you could hire them and drive round the site at 50p for half-an-hour. Sometimes they would 'escape' into the town.

It was a great place, I stayed there for about twelve years. Then I went back to my own trade as an electrician at Micaply. I was made redundant there and eventually they went out of business altogether like the rest of the companies which had set up on the old airfield. The Sunset Inn is the only business established in those years which is still going strong and it was established by a local man without any government grants or anything like that.

The Bachelors on stage at the Sunset Inn.

Sun Set Inn

STANWIX PARK
Holiday Centre
Tel: Silloth 671/2.

Central Focus Point of
The Local
Entertainment Scene

BARRY HOPE
Manager

★ A Different Show each night ★
OPENS AT 7.00 p.m. EACH NIGHT

★ **BINGO** — Monday, 8.30 p.m., Thursday 9.30 p.m.
★ **KIDDIES DISCO** — Tuesday, Thursday, 7.00
★ **DANCING** — Wednesday, Friday, Saturday, Sunday.

The Sunset Inn is open to Holidaymakers and local residents and to ensure a good seat it is necessary to be in the Club by 6.30 on Dance Nights. There is no admission after 10.30 and an extra charge after 10.00 p.m. Chicken and Scampi Meals are available at reasonable prices.

PLEASE ENSURE THAT YOU HAVE MEMBERSHIP CARDS

Silloth Green in the 70s.

The green in 1975. The box-like structure, centre right, was a portakabin which housed the Nat West Bank while their branch was being modernised. The premises in Eden Street re-opened in April 1976. The manager at the time was David Ritchie.

The Gospel Van was a familiar sight on Silloth Green during these years.

Here local songstress, Margaret Shuttleworth is at the microphone for her rendition of 'The Best Book to Read is The Bible'.

A Royal Visit

The princess meets local lass, Margaret Markley, in the Tourist Information Office.
Rev. Tony Miller looks on.

On 7th June 1973, H.R.H. Princess Margaret, The Queen's sister, visited Abbeytown. She opened the new Holm Cultram Arts Centre and, in the evening, attended a gala concert in the Abbey Church.

She landed at Carlisle Airport in the morning and arrived in Abbeytown at 2.30 pm. The vicar, Rev. Anthony Miller, and the Bishop of Carlisle greeted her there. She then entered the church for a service of thanksgiving for the restoration of the abbey. After this, she was presented with a key and opened the new ambulatory which led to the arts centre.

She met the centre's architect, R.P. Gray, and some of the local craftsmen and traders who had been involved in the work and then toured the centre.

She left at 4.30pm for Silloth and relaxed for a while at the newly re-opened Golf Hotel before attending an early evening reception and dinner there. She then returned to Abbeytown for the concert.

The Northern Sinfonia Orchestra, conducted by Eduardo Mata, performed works by Richard Strauss, Elgar and Mozart. They accompanied Stoika Milanova in a Bach Violin Concerto and Peter Frankl for Ravel's Piano Concerto in G.

The Cumberland News music critic gave the performance a luke-warm review, although singling out the pianist for particular praise. He concluded "the splendour of the closing harmonies continued to vibrate in the memory – like the light which, at nearly midnight, still lingered in the Solway sky."

Princess Margaret left just before 11pm and flew back to London that night.

A young Tony Markley leads the choir into the church for the Service of Thanksgiving.

The Holm Cultram Arts Centre

The Rev. Anthony Miller came to Holm Cultram in 1965. He saw the old abbey as an ideal venue for an arts centre. With considerable financial assistance from the county and the Arts Council, he set to work on a pair of dilapidated cottages in the churchyard. He transformed these into a library, meeting rooms, a kitchen, a shop, a bar and a tourist information centre. A newly-built 'ambulatory' joined the cottages to the church. This provided space for refreshments and a display of the abbey's most important relics. Much of the building work was done by local tradesmen on a voluntary basis.

The Arts Festivals

In 1970, Rev. Miller launched the first Holm Cultram Festival of The Arts. A programme of music and drama, linked to a Flower Festival, was held in the abbey during June. It became an annual event. At first, the emphasis was firmly on church music. The Abbey Singers from Carlisle featured together with organ recitals while the Century Theatre Company performed their version of the Lincoln Mystery Play.

By 1973, when Princess Margaret visited, the festival had expanded to a three week programme with over sixteen events. In the second week, the Abbey Singers, conducted by Andrew Sievewright performed "Dunston and the Devil" an opera by Malcolm Williamson. The programme also featured the world premiere of "The Winter Star", a specially commissioned work composed and directed by Williamson who, two years later, was appointed Master of the Queen's Music; a post he held for over twenty-five years.

Also in 1973, a more popular element was added to the Festival programme when Acker Bilk appeared with his Paramount Jazz Band. Over the next few years, almost all of the leading British 'Trad Jazz' bands of the day appeared at Abbeytown, together with a great number of internationally famous classical musicians.

Rev. Tony Miller left the parish in 1976 when he handed over a cheque for £500. He said that, over the past few years, he had made 72 radio broadcasts, written various articles for the press and appeared on TV several times; he had been saving-up the fees from these to present them as a goodbye gift to the church.

A tremendously popular feature of the festivals was what visitors referred to as 'The Bar in the Vestry'

His successor, Rev. Albert Baker, took over as director of the festival. In July 1977, he announced the arts centre was to close and that there would be no more festivals. He said that falling audiences and a reduction in funding from Northern Arts had forced the decision on him but denied the organisation was bankrupt.

Following this, a dedicated band of supporters tried to keep the festival going. They had some success but, by 1979, the festival had shrunk to just one week. The artists came from the local area and the events included a Church Missionary Festival and the youth of Abbeytown performing 'Joseph and his Amazing Technicolor Dream Coat'.

The closure of the Arts Centre makes headline news.

The lasting legacy from these years are the range of buildings, formerly the arts centre, which have provided a home for many community groups and still make a fine back-drop to the Abbey's ancient sculptures and memorials.

Some of the artists who appeared at the festivals

Malcolm Williamson.

Paco Pena (Flamenco Guitar)
Enloc Wu (Piano)
RAF Regiment Band
Acker Bilk and his Paramount Jazz Band
Georgian String Quartet
Terry Lightfoot and his jazz band
Juan Martin (classical guitar).
Felling Male Voice Choir
Kenny Ball and his jazz band
Philip Jones Brass Ensemble
Peter Katin (Piano)

Yehudi Menuhin.

The Munich Chamber Orchestra
Terry Lightfoot and his jazz band
Alex Welsh and his jazz band
John Heddle Nash and his Gilbert & Sullivan company.
Monty Sunshine and his jazz band
Leon Gossens and the Fitzwilliam Quartet
Carlos Bonell (Classical Guitar)
Fou Ts'ong (Piano)
Linden Singers
Stephane Grappelli

Chris Barber and his Jazz Band

*New Vaudeville Jazz Band –
do you remember 'Winchester Cathedral'?*

DAVID HILL

a Carlisle lad, gave his first organ recital at the Arts Centre while still a teenager in 1971.

In 1987, he became Master of Music at Winchester Cathedral and, in 2007, was appointed Chief Conductor of the BBC Singers.

CHAPTER NINE
And Finally . . . .

Throughout the latter part of the century, the cooling towers of the Chapel Cross atomic power station dominated the view over the Solway.

The 1980s and 90s are a little too close at hand to be regarded as history. So, in this chapter, we take only a brief look at these decades and then go on to examine several topics which cover the whole of the twentieth century.

By the 1980s, people were arguably better off than they had ever been. The majority had a car or, at least, the use of one. The welfare state had improved health and removed poverty for most, while home appliances like washing machines and freezers had transformed domestic life. Stereos and videos enhanced home leisure, but at the expense of cinemas and community halls. Technology had changed virtually all aspects of life.

However, the last years of the century were economically unstable. The early 1990s were particularly tough on shops and businesses. A major recession and the withdrawal of grants for industry took their toll. Most of the new firms which had arrived in the 1960s closed their operations; those remaining did so with fewer staff. Local residents who worked at similar businesses in West Cumbria also lost their jobs. At one point, the port of Silloth came very close to closure - concerns that Silloth was 'finished' were high.

In the country, farmers' lives were influenced by the European Common Agricultural Policy; grants and subsidies from Government helped them financially. Farm work, from milking cows to ploughing and harvesting, was done with mechanical help. By now, tractors were everywhere. Large steel framed barns and silos were being put up to house increasing numbers of stock, fodder crops and machinery.

Tourists still came to The Plain, but caravans and chalets had replaced boarding houses; the remaining hotels were only just hanging on. Holiday camps became ever more sophisticated but had to compete with foreign holidays, which were now within reach of almost everyone, and very popular. Even in the 'the season' Silloth's beach, promenade and Green were usually deserted, prompting various initiatives to bring visitors back.

There was increasing concern and interest in the natural environment. Measures were taken to protect the landscape and wildlife of this area, which had been declared an Area of Outstanding Natural Beauty.

Two organisations, The Solway Firth Partnership and Solway Rural Initiative, were formed to preserve the environment and assist communities.

Stephen Wright remembers.......

As a child, I would spend days out and holidays with my grandparents at Silloth. They had a chalet on the Stanwix field in Blitterlees. Silloth in the 1980s seemed very quiet as far as visitors were concerned – the West Beach was usually deserted and it was hard to imagine the hordes of trippers that used to spill out from the train until the 60s. Although the holidaymakers were absent, there was much commercial activity going on and that was far more interesting to me.

The docks were one of my favourite places and, in the 80s, there was quite a lot going on. Grain ships called at the mill where the wheat was sucked out by vacuum into the huge silo tower at one end – this was Silloth's main landmark, made even more visible by the fact that it was painted bright green! Cattle ships also visited, usually the 'Tynedale One' and I remember watching the cattle walk off the ship and into the lairage. Blue Circle Cement had a terminal at the docks with three storage tanks that could also be seen for miles around. A smart little ship called the 'Mercurius' would come in to load the powder for ports in the Isle of Man.

Various bulk and packaged cargo was handled, such as animal fodder, cement clinker, peat moss and milk products from Nestles at Dalston. I enjoyed watching the stevedores, D. A. Harrison, loading and unloading the ships with various cranes, forklift trucks, shovels and lorries all working on the dockside. On one occasion my grandfather asked if we could go on board a ship and the ship's mate agreed. It was a dream come true and I was quite excited as we walked up the gangway from the quay and onto the main deck. The cargo was bulk animal fodder, which had a strong but not unpleasant odour and we all stood looking into the hold as grabfuls of the pellets were lifted out and emptied into a hopper.

Sometimes there were as many as four ships in port and, if we were lucky, we might see one arrive or depart.

The docks, the flour mill and the factories on the airfield kept Silloth a busy place and there were a lot of trucks on the roads. You would see the yellow cement tankers, the green Carrs flour tankers, Harrisons' blue lorries and many others all around Silloth.

Harrison's trucks.

Stephen at the chalet field, Blitterlees, 1983

Boom and Bust

The Micaply factory from the air.

The MAS Management Team model a fine range of executive clothing in 1990.

Despite beginning with a recession, the 1980s were a time of industrial expansion and enterprise.

In 1981 Yates, formerly known as Printing Techniques, opened a large £6 million factory at Silloth. They took on thirty-eight new trainees, and employed 150 people, making copper conducting material for electronic goods. Built on the site of a hangar next to the main road, this was the largest building ever constructed on the Solway Plain and contrasted with the surrounding architecture. Yates was to prosper during this decade thanks to the local workforce.

Nearby, Micaply continued to manufacture the material from which circuit boards were made, with a staff of 130. In 1984 a restructuring of the

company led to the name of MAS being used.

Cheri foam and Curled Hair prospered. A new £1 million moulding line was installed there. The foam and hair plants employed 100 staff between them. In 1981, Carnation took on thirty more staff and were busy. Many of the people employed in these large concerns came from the West Cumbrian towns. Special buses took them to and from work.

Carrs continued to prosper and diversify. As well as their busy flour and animal feed mills, they opened a fertiliser blending plant in former RAF Hangars near Wath farm. They began importing some of the ingredients from overseas, bringing more ships into Silloth dock.

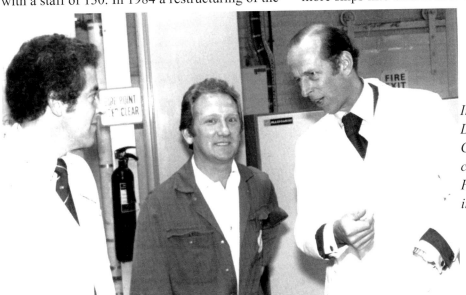

In 1981, H.R.H. The Duke of Kent visited Carrs Mill. Here he is chatting with George Howe and Ivan Wallace in the Cubing Plant.

Meanwhile, on the land at Silloth once occupied by the chemical works, Philip Harker was developing an industrial estate. He had begun a vehicle salvaging and scrap operation there, and a firm of animal feed suppliers was there too, in the old Fisons sheds. Several new industrial units were also built by English Estates, near the docks.

Local people were also setting up small enterprises, aided by grants from central government. Among the people to benefit were Rolf and Moira Knoery of New Cowper. They received a grant under the COSIRA scheme run by the Rural Development Commission, which was for making use of derelict or redundant buildings. They had turned disused farm buildings into a workshop where they would restore old vehicles. Not only that, but theirs was the 150th grant given out since the scheme began. This landmark led to the cheque being presented to them by deputy Prime Minister, Willie Whitelaw.

This bubble of expansion burst in October 1987, when the world financial system crashed in a dramatic fashion.

It was the start of a fall which became one of the worst economic crises of the century.

Coulthard's Concrete Products.

The early 1990s were very difficult for manufacturing and retail. The recession and the ending of government grants meant that, one by one, the enterprises which had set up in Silloth shut down.

Cheri foam and curled hair ceased production in 1991. After being taken over by a Luxembourg concern and re-named Circuit Foil (UK), the big Yates plant closed in 1993. Carnation of Cumberland closed down in the mid-1990s. The remaining factories struggled along with fewer staff and uncertain futures.

Carrs had mixed fortunes. In 1998 the animal feed mill ceased production due to new policy on the proximity of feed milling to residential areas. It was demolished, leaving the mills half the size they were. Production was moved to a site near Carlisle.

Their flour milling did well after celebrity cook Delia Smith recommended their products. People went out and bought the flour, leading to increased production and recognition.

By the end of the century, industrial activity was much smaller than it had been a decade earlier.

The exception was a new arrival called ENKEV. This Dutch enterprise made filling for upholstery using natural fibres including horsehair. With local skills and knowledge remaining from the Cumberland Curled Hair workforce, a new plant was set up in the station road trading units at Silloth. Later, it moved to the former Carnation premises on the old Airfield.

The former Yates building seen after closure in 1993..

A Glimpse of the 80s and 90s

A miniature railway on Silloth Green was a big hit with the kids in the 80s.

Horses from Allonby Riding School.

Allonby in the 90s.

Christchurch Choir with Rev. Francis Tompkins and organist, Mr Cullen.

Launch of the 'Ship of Dreams' made by children from Silloth school. East Cote slipway. May 1994.

In the limelight . . .

During the 1980s, the Silloth Amateur Operatic Society mounted a series of spectacular productions in the school hall. Each Christmas they presented a pantomime. The profits from this financed the costume hire for the following year's Gilbert and Sullivan operetta.

Silloth readers can have fun spotting friends and family under the make-up!

Above: 'The Gondoliers'

Below: 'Iolanthe'

'HMS Pinafore'

'Cinderella'

'The Mikado'

Dockside.....

Container ship 'Tequila Sunrise', one of the largest vessels ever to visit Silloth, leaving for El Salvador in 1987.

By the 1980s, things had changed in the port of Silloth. Only a handful of people worked there regularly – the Harbour Master, (Capt. John Myers), four dock gate men (Colin Akitt Snr., Colin Akitt Jnr, Cyril Akitt and George Selkirk) along with a waterman (Malcolm Fisher) who got fresh water onto the ships.

In 1980, cargoes consisted of wheat, brought on coasters, cattle from Ireland and occasional loads of Molasses. There were no exports. However things were to change quite dramatically. Within a few years the port was going through one of its busiest and most interesting periods.

Local Haulier, D.A. Harrison, built new storage facilities on land leased from the port authority. These included a large warehouse, a set of bulk storage tanks, a weighbridge and office. His company also became the port's licensed

The docks in June 1985. 'Mercurius' has loaded cement powder for Ramsey, Isle of Man, while the 'Fenja' has brought grass pellets from Denmark.

Stevedore, taking over cargo handling work, plus haulage and storage. Wheat continued to be unloaded by Carr's staff at the mill, and Tynedale handled the cattle.

New customers arrived. Blue Circle began using the dock to ship cement powder in bulk and on pallets. They used Harrisons facilities to store the products before it was shipped. Bulk powder went to the Isle of Man, bags went to the Scottish Hebrides and cement clinker was shipped to Magheramorne in Ireland.

Nestles also came in. They sent milk-based foods, made at their Cumbrian creamery, to the Middle East, and later Central America. These palletised wares were put on larger ships for the long distance voyage. Animal feeds and fertilisers, mainly for Carrs, began to arrive from across Europe. Imports also included peat moss and paper pulp For a time, scrap metal was also exported. By the mid-1980s, 100,000 tons of cargo was going through the port annually.

A modern office and operations block was built by the port authority. The long-established shipping agency, Stronachs, continued its important role with their agent, John Hayhurst.

Sadly, this busy situation was reversed as a recession followed the financial crash at the end of 1987. Traffic dropped away steeply.

A new harbour master, Captain Chris Puxley, arrived in 1990 to a sadly idle port. Shortly after his appointment, a senior official from his employers, Associated British Ports, paid a visit to Silloth. Traffic was about the lowest in the port's history, and the official doubted it had a future. He thought the best option was to concentrate on yachts and leisure, and forget cargo ships. Chris disagreed. This part of the Solway never saw yachts. The tidal range, currents and sandbanks made it unpopular with leisure mariners.

He and others instead sought out new customers and advertised the port. The improving economic climate aided their quest and, by the middle of the decade, traffic was steady again. As well as an increase in the traditional cargoes – grain, fertiliser and cement – the port saw shipments of palm kernels from Nigeria, and live fish, going from breeding ponds in Cumbria to fish farms in Scotland, where they would grow to full size. The docks ended the century quite busy, with the average size of ships and cargoes continuing to increase.

The dredger 'Welsh Dolphin' working at the port in 1995 with Colin Akitt Junr on the quay.
Colin had worked at the docks since the 1960s.

Schooling the century

In 1900, almost all of the children in our area received their entire education in one of the village schools. The official school-leaving age was fourteen but many children were permitted to leave at twelve or thirteen, especially if an extra pair of hands was needed on the family's farm. Some middle-class families paid for their boys to attend the Grammar Schools in Wigton or Carlisle. A few lucky girls were sent to the High School in Carlisle or the Thomlinson School in Wigton. The County awarded a limited number of 'scholarships' to these schools for children from poorer families. In Wigton, the co-educational Quaker Friends' School was popular with the more prosperous farmers; it took both boarders and day-scholars. There were several small private schools in the area.

For a few years, just after the Second World War, there was a Catholic school in Skinburness.

St Joseph's was located in Hymer House and was run by Sisters of the Order of Mercy from Wigton. It catered for boys and girls of all ages. In addition to the normal subjects, the Sisters also taught typing, shorthand and other commercial subjects.

After the First World War, the official leaving-age of fourteen was imposed by the government with a provision for an extra two years of free education if desired. This move was unpopular with employers, parents and the kids themselves. In 1947, the age for leaving school was again raised to fifteen and the eleven-plus examination was introduced. This meant that the brighter children got a free place in one of the Grammar Schools while the rest stayed on at the local all-age school or went to one of the new Secondary Modern Schools in Wigton or Silloth.

Allonby School Group, about 1916

Woodwork Class,
Holme St Cuthbert's School, 1950s.

Aldoth School, 1925.

Silloth Secondary School

In May 1937, the Cumberland Education Committee approved plans for a new secondary school at Silloth. This would accommodate senior pupils from the old all-ages school. The old buildings, later to become the Heritage Centre, would continue to house the infants and juniors.

In the spring of 1938, the committee invited tenders and awarded the building contract to John Twiname of Brigham at a total cost of £22,703.16.5d.

In July 1939, the Education Committee reported that work had begun and that "it may be claimed fairly to be a pattern in modern school building." It then went on to note "Other plans were approved by the board but, of course, all progress has been checked by the subsequent developments in the international situation".

By this time, construction of the new RAF airfield was well advanced. By the following autumn, activity there had reached a point where the Director of Education "thought it wise to close the Silloth and Colt Park Schools with regard to their proximity to the aerodrome". Both schools closed and the RAF used them as billets.

In November 1940, the committee made arrangements with Cumberland Motor Services for "the conveyance of displaced scholars to and from Wigton Elementary School at fifty shillings per double-decker per day". The Air Ministry declined to grant the committee anything toward this expenditure.

The Silloth children received a half-day's education at Wigton. The Wigton kids got the other half!

Despite the great difficulties in obtaining building materials during the war, the new school was completed by July 1940 but then the Chairman and Vice Chairman of County Council agreed to authorise the Air Ministry "to take possession of Silloth New Senior Council School. To be returned at the end of the war in the same condition even if, in the meantime, it had been damaged by enemy action".

The school was used to accommodate airmen for the rest of the war. The hall became the camp's cinema and, occasionally, live shows were also presented there.

It was only after the war ended that all the pupils moved in. The Education Committee struggled for years to get the Air Ministry to pay-up for the damage they had caused to the building during their occupation and to remove the camouflage paint they had applied to the exterior.

The School in 1949.

The Class of 1948/49
Traces of the camouflage paint can still be seen on the school walls.

FRONT ROW: (left to right) Boo Little, Joey Baxter, Malcolm Harrison, Wilson Connor, Colin Bonner, Bobby Sutton, Alan Borland, Jim Dockeray, George Scoular, John Graham, Kenmere Marshall, Hughie Scott.

SECOND ROW: Shirley Lamb, Eileen Smith, Isabel Underwood, Audrey France, Dorothy Johnstone, Beryl Griffeths, Irene Riddick, Geoffrey Lightfoot, Anita Fletcher, Elsie Messenger, Joyce Brough, Marian Walker, Connie Bennett, Dorothy Henderson.

THIRD ROW: Freddie Cooper, Jean Bennett, Joan Wise, Marjorie Pearson, Ann Hall, Mavis Watts, Irene Stitt, Eileen Baskerville, Marjorie Gass, Rosemary Spooner, Jean Reed, Betty Brown, Milly Faulder, Evelyn Hedley, Jim Graham.

BACK ROW: Harold Bosward, Unknown, Ray Penrice, John Brough, Derek Gass, Alan Wise, Graeme Batey, Kenny Dixon, Ronnie Wells, Gordon Strickland, Barry Chapel, John Slack, Eddie Hodgson, Cliff Little.

Geoff Watson

The 1944 Education act provided not only free secondary education for all children but also established a system of grants for those wishing to go on to Higher Education. An early beneficiary of the act was Geoff Watson from Salta, near Mawbray.

Geoff passed his 11plus exam in 1957 and went to the Nelson Thomlinson Grammar School in Wigton. In 1965, he received a grant from the County Education Committee and also a small amount from the Longcake Charity to continue his studies. He took a four year course at Grey College, part of Durham University, and obtained a B.A. degree and a Teacher's Certificate.

He taught French and sports at Trinity School in Carlisle until he retired in 1993. He was the first local lad from Holme St Cuthberts School ever to go to university.

Geoff in his brand new Nelson-Thom blazer, at Durham and after graduation.

Shops and shopkeepers

William Longcake in the ice cream shop at West Silloth

Walton's Saturday Girls: Jane Briggs, Beverley Shaw, Angela Robertson, Alison Aird, Pauline Johnston and Sharon Robertson, in the doorway.

Berry's Bakery in the mid 1980s.

Davina Walton's drapery store in Silloth.

Allonby's old post office.

The Ritz

Bill Brown ran the Ritz Cafe in Station Road, Silloth for many years together with the toy and fancy goods shop next door. He was also chairman of the Chamber of Commerce and played a leading role in the campaign to keep the rail line open.

The hut on West Beach

Frying every night

Throughout the century it was possible to buy Fish and Chips at No.12, Solway St., Silloth.

Elizabeth Brough began as a 'fried fish dealer' around 1903. By 1911, it had passed to Joseph Zanelli, the first of the 'foreigners' to run the shop. Around 1923, Spaniard, Salvador Bilbao, took over. During the 1930s, it was held by Jenara Munoz and family. The Trespaderne family moved there from another shop in Silloth around 1947 and brothers, Juan and Jose, ran it as a very popular cafe and takeaway shop for the next 40 years. They retired in the 1980s, but the business continued as 'The Crispy Cod' and, by 1995, 'The Solway Fryer'.

Bill with his assistant, Noreen Littleton.

The Ritz had a branch located near West Beach. The hut they used had originally been built as a shelter for Sister Lilly who organised trips to the seaside for under-privileged children from Carlisle.

Wilson Robinson "Pop" Carr and his garage in Waver Street, Silloth.

Clay Dabbins (or Daubins)

As agriculture became more mechanised, far fewer men were needed on the farms; those who remained now lived in council houses. This had one, sad side effect: the demolition of the last of the 'Clay Dabbins' – a part of our heritage that has vanished without trace. These single-storey cottages were built of clay and wattle, around a cruck frame, made from tree trunks, with a foundation of cobbles from the sea shore. They had housed the families who worked the land, probably since the tenth century. By the late 1950s, few were still used as homes – most had been converted into hen houses or implement stores. Later, even these were replaced with modern, pre-fabricated structures. Nobody had the foresight to preserve one.

These pictures of Brownrigg Cottage, near Seaville, during its demolition in September 1954, clearly show the method of construction.

The cottages beside the pub in Mawbray were among the last to survive as homes.

Canvas, caravans and chalets

Enjoying an al fresco meal, Solway holiday camp, Blitterlees around 1950.

By the 1950s, camping was fast becoming the most popular type of holiday on the Solway Plain. The first signs of it had appeared in the 1930s. On the banks between Maryport and Silloth, caravans and huts started to appear as summer residences for people from nearby towns.

Saltpans was the oldest camp in the area. It was begun early in the century by the Robertson family who lived in the cottages there. It was looked after for most of its life by Hannah Fisher (née Robertson) who stayed there all her life. It was popular, and a variety of caravans and chalets were sited on both sides of the coast road. Some nestled among the old salt workings. Campers got their water from a pump and used chemical toilets, enjoying the position between 'Bluebell' hill and the shore.

Many farmers saw the financial benefits of this new enterprise and, by 1960, almost every village on the coast had a holiday camp. Allonby led the way with three sites. The Misses Elsie and Kitty Saul of Crookhurst ran the oldest one at Vicarage Field, plus another on Walker's field, north of the village. Eric and Mary Williamson ran the Dickinson place camp while relatives, William and Mary Williamson, ran one at Spring Lea. Percy Foster of Greenlaw House also had one at the north end of the village. Later, in the 60s, came Bobby Watson's 'Fellview' caravan site, Mr Sanderson's 'Westville' and the Twentyman's field next to the

Westnewton road. All were well-used. Blitterlees had three camps: 'Moordale', run by Stan Earnshaw, and two more run by Hilton Stanwix.

These camps were created by the campers themselves – the farmers merely allowed them to put accommodation there, and took their money. Government Sanitary regulations forced them to put fresh water and toilets on site, but in these early days, nothing more was done.

East Cote, near Skinburness, had its first camp in the 1930s, run by Norman Harryman. After the war, there were two camping sites at East Cote, one run by Nick and Marjorie Littleton who farmed there, and 'Glenpark', which was managed by James and Mabel Mackenzie of Carlisle.

Robert Lightfoot began the Silloth farm caravan park. Unlike the other proprietors he provided modern, static caravans; by 1970 there were over 100. He retired in the early 70s when the park was taken over by Clarksons Caravans. In 1982, it was sold to Eric Stanwix who renamed it Hylton Park. This site occupied fields to the east of the town which had, originally, been a training and accommodation site for airmen. Some of the caravans bordered the railway line; this gave an extra bonus to young boys who could watch the trains pass their holiday home.

Some of the early sites

Saltpans.

Percy Foster's field at Allonby

Glenpark was situated just off Skinburness Road

The Silloth Farm Site in the early 60s.

The ex-RAF huts, occupied by the squatters, can be seen on the extreme right.

In later years, this site became known as 'Hylton Park'.

The 'Solway Holiday Camp'

The Stanwix brothers, Hilton and Walter, farmed at Blitterlees. In the 1930s, many Carlisle people were coming down to Silloth and camping with tents so the brothers set aside a field for them.

During Race Week and other holidays, lots came with their tents and made use of it. More permanent structures then began to appear – people brought on huts, rail and road carriages, and caravans. More fields were taken over as the demand grew.

Carr and Henderson family bakery.

People applied to erect chalets on the fields. These chalets were built of wood, (some recycled from other buildings) and some had brick chimneys for a coal fire. Residents cooked on gas stoves and bottled gas also provided lighting and heating.

In the early days, a mix of all sorts of structures existed on the camp, which was known simply as Stanwix's field. They were added to and enhanced over the years and each was unique. Some were given names and many were erected by individuals who then sub-let them to families for a term. Residents often got together and organised their own games and entertainment.

The early caravans and chalets had character and were homely, with a charm of their own, something lost as manufactured, static models were adopted. As more people bought their cars, space for private, touring caravans was provided on the sites.

In 1947, Hilton Stanwix had bought a field owned by the District Council. At one end was a house, built as a cottage hospital in 1902. It ceased to be a hospital in 1935 but, because of this, the field was sometimes known as the hospital field.

Hilton intended to develop a camp of purpose-built chalets. Over the next 10 years, individuals erected about fifty wooden chalets round the edge of the field. All had names, such as 'Sea Wind', 'Meadows End' and 'Hawthorn Cottage'. The only services consisted of communal taps and toilets. However, in 1951, shortly after the camp appeared, Jessie Carr started a small bakery and shop between the camp and the coast road. Over the years it provided bread, cakes and pies to those living and visiting nearby, the delicious fare being very popular and making some very happy campers!

In 1965, after Hilton passed away, his two sons Roland and Eric took over the running of the site. They gave up farming and concentrated on developing 'The Stanwix Park Holiday Centre'. Along with their sons and daughters, they invested much effort in the site, transforming it with new accommodation and facilities.

Gone were the old chalets and vehicle bodies, replaced with purpose-made static caravans and, from 1980, some continental-style apartments. Outdoors, campers could use the swimming pool, adventure play area, take pony treks and ride the unusual four wheel 'cyclo-mobiles' around the site. Inside, the modern Sunset Entertainment Centre offered campers and locals a variety of live and recorded music nights, together with bars, lounge areas, dance floors and amusements.

The centre was refurbished at a cost of £200,000 in 1988, by which time the Club had 2,000 members. It now offered seating for 600 people, had extensive catering facilities plus an impressive state of the art lighting and sound system. A further development was carried out for the 1996 season, consisting of a new leisure centre and indoor pool, a bowling alley and refurnished restaurant and lounges.

As well as this main centre, the Stanwix family continued to operate 'Hylton Park' on the eastern edge of town and, at Blitterlees, the field of chalets next to the old hospital house remained as it was, giving a simpler and quieter holiday for those who liked it that way.

STANWIX PARK HOLIDAY CENTRE, SILLOTH

The Camping Coaches

Cowboys and Indians was the universal children's game in the 50s and 60s.

There was another type of self-catering holiday; from 1956, visitors could choose to book a holiday at one of British Railways' camping coaches.

These had been introduced in the 1930s and could be found all over the country at popular tourist locations. They were ordinary rail carriages placed on sidings and fitted out for living instead of travelling. In 1956, four were brought to Silloth and left in a siding near the beach. For the next eight years, they provided holiday accommodation for families from all over the North of England and Scotland, and were advertised at various stations on the rail network. Sadly, these had to be removed when the railway closed in 1964.

Local people also enjoyed camping. Three Mawbray Lads, David Allan, Colin Thompson and Malcolm Osborn enjoy a gourmet treat with the local youth club in the Lake District.

The Lido

Early caravan and chalet on the Lido site.

In 1962, Stenton Hodgson, a Carlisle businessman, bought a large area of the former RAF base. Hodgson was in the caravan sales trade, and intended to establish a caravan park there.

Before long, the site was up and running with Bruce Johnston as manager and Richard Faunch as Camp Warden. Offering a range of modern, static caravans plus areas for touring vans and tents, it contrasted with some other camps – there were no old bus bodies or huts here.

At first, it was just a caravan site with basic facilities, but Hodgson had grander plans in mind. In the late 60s, he spent £250,000 turning it into a Holiday/Leisure park.

It reopened in 1969 as the Solway Lido holiday centre. Facilities included a leisure centre containing a club, dance hall, bars, restaurant and a heated swimming pool. There was also a small supermarket, launderette, games room and children's play area. The new centre employed quite a big team of staff to run all the facilities.

As well as 200 static caravans, 60 modern chalets had been built and there was plenty of ground for touring vans and tents.

Success and failure

The new Lido was an instant hit, seeing 4,000

campers over the Whit Weekend in 1969 with cars queuing to get in. Over the next few years, the amount of accommodation was increased as campers from all over the North of England and Scotland descended on it.

Susan Denard remembers these early times: "People say the Lido is popular now, but it's nothing like it was back then. They were queuing to get onto the site; we got people from all over. For a while, coachloads of Asian families used to come from Birmingham at Easter. A man called Raj Patel used to organise these. A lot of the chalets would be packed.

"Lots of Glaswegians used to come here during Glasgow Holiday Week and from Newcastle too. There was plenty going on – some of the things I can't really repeat here!"

SOLWAY LIDO
SPECIAL EASTER OFFER
Hire a Luxury Caravan or Chalet for Easter Weekend for £4 inclusive of Full Facilities and Club House, Lounge, etc.
NEW this Year —— CATERING in RESTAURANT and SNACKBAR by PIONEER of CARLISLE
Call, phone or write for free details now
Caravan Owners : Sites available for Private use or Letting Agency

An advert for the Lido as it was in 1965.

Organised entertainment was a big feature on the camp. In addition to the live music, cabaret and other acts which played at the Tipple Inn and Lido Club, there were discos for teens and adults. Indoor games and competitions were organised; girls could enter the annual Miss Solway Lido contest. The camp was on the doorstep for the 'Helldrivers' meetings and other events. These brought huge numbers of customers in the 1970s, which some regard as the camp's heyday.

The Tipple Inn staff in 1974.

In fact the Lido became too popular. In 1971, representatives of the District Council held a meeting with Messrs Hodgson, Johnston and Sutcliffe of Border Developments, the company behind the camp. They were investigating overcrowding issues. During bank holiday breaks, more touring campers had been allowed on than the camp was meant for. The management were told to address this as they were creating a health and safety problem. On top of this, seventy residents of Skinburness Road had complained about noise from loudspeakers on the camp and had delivered a petition to the council.

By the 1980s the Solway Lido holiday park was considered the premier camp in the county; it offered more entertainment than any other site. It hosted a number of special events. Every May a 'Family Festival' was staged which featured visiting celebrities amongst them, Jon Pertwee and children's TV presenters Keith Chegwin and Maggie Philbin.

'Maytime' the 1982 Lido Festival.

In 1983, the Lido hosted a motorsport rally and, in 1984, world BMX freestyle champion, Eddie Fiola, appeared and impressed the crowds with his bike stunts. The last show, in 1986, included helicopter rides, an army display performance and fashion show.

The camp itself had been given a facelift. Now the centre had a continental theme. Visitors could enjoy the 'Toledo Noveau' nightclub, new bars, and 'Cafe Continental'. Children had the new Teddyland play centre and everybody could use the new Cuebowl games centre. On top of this, there were new indoor and outdoor swimming pools and outdoor play areas. The improvements had cost over £100,000.

Everything appeared rosy on the surface. Few people expected the news that Border Developments had called in the receivers at the end of 1987. Accountants, Price Waterhouse of Newcastle, took over their assets which, as well as the Lido, included another holiday camp at Saltcoats in Ayrshire, plus the caravan sales business in Carlisle. The camps remained open and popular while a new owner was sought.

This didn't take long. In March a deal was set up with property and leisure group Dyke Brothers, based at Windermere. This company had also recently purchased the Skinburness Hotel. At first, things went well but the increasingly weak economic situation caused problems and, in October 1990, the receivers were called in again. This time, finding a buyer for the camp took much longer. After two years, it was finally taken over by the Hagan group, an Irish leisure company which continued to operate it for the rest of the century.

. . . and elsewhere

In the early 1990s the Williamson family of Spring Lea farm opened Allonby's equivalent of Stanwix Park. A striking building was erected housing a swimming pool, leisure centre and restaurant. It was used by their many static and touring caravan customers as well as the local community.

The impressive gateway to the Lido, seen in 1993, a year after being taken on by the Hagan group.

By the 1980s, there were more than twenty licensed holiday sites on the Solway Plain. Most were on the coast, from Blue Dial up to Skinburness but a handful, such as Manor House near Edderside and Tarnside near Mawbray, were inland. These camps were popular but, as holidays abroad became affordable, the crowds which had descended on them in the 1950s and 60s tailed off. It became almost embarrassing for many Carlisle families to visit Silloth when they could now go to Majorca, Tenerife or Florida. This trend had a very noticeable impact on Silloth; its Green, promenade and West Beach were now quiet, even on summer weekends.

Ray Johnston at the Lido with a group of exchange students from Lexington, Massachusetts, USA and their Silloth partners in 1975. Is that John Denver, second from right?

Staff Snap Album

A Special Lido Buffet

Colin Pearson, June Johnston, Michael Pearson and Paul Hesketh outside the Lido Chip Shop. Early 70s

Raymond Johnston on the Lido tractor.

Paul Hesketh and June Johnston staff the snackbar.

A hundred years at Swinsty

Swinsty around 1910. Note John Hurst's initials on the wall.

In the early years of the Century, the *West Cumberland Times* featured a regular column called 'Cracks with West Coast Farmers'. The author, who signed himself 'Cross Fleury', visited a different farm each week and described its buildings, livestock, crops and farming methods. In 1919, he visited Swinsty in Abbeytown. At that time, the tenant was John Hurst.

In 1933, Jonathan Mattinson took over the tenancy and his son George, together with his wife Ivy, and brother, Robert, continued to farm there until 1997. Using the original article and George's memories it has been possible to trace the changes in agriculture over almost the entire twentieth century.

Previously at Swinsty

The farm has a long and fascinating history. Its name is derived from the 'Swine Sty' where the monks from Holm Cultram Abbey kept their pigs. Henry VIII closed the monastery down in 1538 and its lands became a royal manor. It is thought the first stone farmhouse on the site was built in 1667 using stone from the old abbey. It became the home of James Jackson who, after the English Civil War, acted as bailiff for the manor during the Commonwealth years.

Queen Elizabeth I had given Swinsty, along with several other parcels of land, to the 'Sixteen Men' of Holm Cultram. This group acted as a sort of local parliament and also had responsibility for maintaining the Sea Dyke which protected the coastal areas from the sea.

When the County Council took over responsibility for the dyke, the lands belonging to the Sixteen Men were put into a trust known as the 'Sea Dyke Charity'. Subsequently, the charity sold off much of its land but retained Swinsty where it is still the landlord. The income from the farm's rents has, over the years, provided grants to help many local students through college and university.

An aerial view of the farm in the 1960s. The long building with the pitched roof in the centre of the photograph is the original clay barn. A Dutch barn, used for storing hay can be seen on the left.

In 1919, Swinsty is described as "a ring fence-farm of 125 acres" – all the land in cultivation adjoined the farm buildings. George Mattinson reckons the true acreage was nearer to 97; the rest being low-lying moss land, liable to flooding. During his time there, George added around another 70 acres to the farm. This was land he purchased for himself; it never belonged to the land lords and provided a valuable nest-egg for his retirement. The first field he bought cost £800 and he sold a small slice of it for two building sites – at a very considerable profit. He left a gate and a narrow entry into the field alongside the bungalows which were built there. The owners complained that the cows used to lick their windows as they passed by. George, a canny businessman, agreed to sell them this strip for £1,000. He used his tractor to knock a hole in the wall and make a new entry. He then carried on expanding the estate until he left.

The pattern of crops at Swinsty changed surprisingly little over the century. At its start, the Hursts had around 40 acres of corn and wheat; at its end the Mattinsons had around 30 acres under the plough, mostly of barley. Both families grew potatoes and turnips. In 1919, the potato varieties used were Arran Chief and Great Scot. These were 'old fashioned' by the time George took over; he used Arran Pilots for the early crop and Marris Piper for later on in the year. The turnips were always used as fodder during the autumn for the lambs being fattened for the Christmas markets.

The greatest changes over the years occurred in dairy farming. In 1919, the Hursts had 40 head of cattle of which 10 were 'milkers'. In the winter months, the number being milked was reduced by half as fodder became scarce. When George sold up in 1997, he had 140 head of which 60 or 70

The new Cattle Shed. George Mattinson kept a Charolais bull; most of his herd were Charolais-Friesian crosses.

Ivy Mattinson poses in front of the cowshed wall. The old buildings demolished to make way for the shed contained many stones which had originally formed part of the abbey buildings. These were all preserved and used to build the new structure.

The farm was very busy during the war years. George had two German POWs to help out and found them to be excellent workers. There was a small army training camp at Abbeytown and he supplied it with milk. He was also able to use the NAFFI stores there to obtain a few scarce luxuries for the family – the chief of these being chocolate! He thinks some of the other local farmers made a fortune during these years selling eggs on the black market although, of course, he never did anything like that himself.

were milked all year round. The Hursts had three separate cow byers with between four and ten stalls each. Over the years, the Mattinsons had converted these buildings and added a new 30-stall byre. The milk was collected by a bulk tanker from the Milk Marketing Board dairy at Aspatria. The tanker held 1,500 gallons and called daily. Quite often it overflowed with the huge amount of milk George's herd had produced! In the 1990s, the Sea Dyke Charity demolished many of the old buildings and built a fine new cattle shed which could hold the entire herd of beef cattle for fattening.

In the early years of the century, liquid milk was a difficult commodity to sell. There were problems with the lack of refrigeration and transporting it to the large centres of population.

Because of this, butter was the most profitable product for the Hursts. The *West Cumberland Times* article notes that the dairy at Swinsty contained a barrel churn, a 50-gallon Lister separator and some beautiful briquettes ready for market. The family moulded 40 or 50 pounds each week in summer and about half that quantity in winter. By the time George and Ivy took over, the production of 'farm butter' had virtually ceased and Ivy never got involved with it. She did keep a few hens in the early years but gave these up after the tax man refused to believe her figures regarding their lack of profitability!

In 1919, the Hursts had five working horses including two pedigree mares one of which had just produced 'a most promising foal'. The Mattinsons bought their first tractor just after the war. It was a Ford with spade lugs on the wheels rather than tyres. It cost £157, second hand, from the County Garage at Carlisle.

The first tractor George and Robert bought on their own account cost about £10,000. After three years, it was replaced at a cost of £15,000 by another. Both were Czech manufactured Zetor machines. After retirement George and Ivy moved to a fine Victorian house in Silloth town centre where they lived surrounded by photographs and mementoes of their years at Swinsty. The tiny garden produced the best hanging baskets and floral displays in town.

George in retirement.

SUNNY SILLOTH By Ethel Fisher, MBE

Noo-a-days, aw sorts uv things
Ur miad tu keep us weel,
Pills un aw concoctions
Dependin hoo yu feel.
Bit tu my way uv thinken
Yu can scop awt pills away,
Yu'll fin it duz yu far mare good
Tu come tu Silloth for t'day.

Yu can gaa alang oor prominard
Frae daybreek till neet,
Paddle in oor Solway watter
Un ease yur achen feet.
Git a greet big icecream cornet
That'll mak yu lik yur lips
An, if yur varra ungry,
Theirs sum super fish and chips.

T'shops ur full ur fancy tackle
Fer tu tak sum presents yam;
Sweetshops, bakers, paper shops
And butchers sellun ham.
Swing boats, a bouncy castle,
Un a grand laal kiddies train.
Amusement hall wid Bingo
If it happen cum on rain.

A bonny church an a few laal chapels
At welcoms yan an aw,
A grassy green where't kids can lake
An kick aroon a baw.
Super sands ta lig on, sek castles yu can build
Try oor Solway breezes an git yer lungs weel fillt.

Sum fwoks like tu gaa abroad
Tu Benidrom un Spain,
Thu reckon it'll du them gud
An ease their ivery pain.
But Silloth's ivevry bit as nice
Wid views ower t'Scottish ills,
Just tack it frae me,
Yu'll fergit aboot swallerin pills!

The view from Bessie Winter's window in the 1990s. A final tribute..

ACKNOWLEDGEMENTS

We would like to express our thanks to these people for giving us their help...

Gordon Akitt

Pat Antolak

Joan Armstrong

Lois Baird

John Barker

Mrs W Barker

Jack Baxter

Jack Beake

Jim Bell

Geoff Bland

John Brennan

Robert Carr

Richard Crowe

Keith Dagwell

Susan Denard

Liz Elliott

Mr & Mrs Philip Ferguson

Bob Gibson

Stan Graham

Roger Gullen

Dan Henderson

Barry Hope

Sue Holland

John Huggon

Dennis Irwin

Joe Hope

Betty Kent

Eric Laws

S.E. Lee

Iris Little

Marjorie Littleton

John Lowe

Lawrence & Mary Marshall

Mr & Mrs G. Mattinson

Joan Palmer

Barbara Pegram

Denis Perriam

Gus Proud

Tom Stanwix

Felix Stirling

Carol Stoddart

Wayne Stoddart

John Stronach

Richard Thomas

Martin Tognarelli

Ivan Wallace

Davina Walton

Bobby Watson

Carolyn Williamson

Elaine Wilson

Harry Wilson

Ken Winter

Heather and Olive Wood

Tom Wood

. . . . and everybody we forgot to mention!

Plus the staff and volunteers at............

Helena Thompson Museum, Workington

Carlisle Library

Cumbria Archives (Carlisle)

Cumbria's Regimental Museum

206 Squadron Coastal Command Website

Associated British Ports, Silloth

Carrs Flour Mill, Silloth

Silloth Tourist Information Centre

BIBLIOGRAPHY

Much of this book has been compiled from Contemporary reports found in the pages of:

The Carlisle Journal, Cumberland News, West Cumberland Times and *Wigton Advertiser.*

Minute books and other records from various local authorities were also consulted.

The authors will be delighted to supply detailed references to anyone wishing to undertake further research on any of the topics covered.

The following publications were also used and provide excellent background reading:-

Dictionary of National Biography

Chris Puxley: The Port of Silloth 1859-2009 (Bernard McCall, 2009)

Marshall Hall: The Artists of Northumbria (Marshall Hall Associates, 1982)

Margaret Forster: Rich Desserts and Captain's Thin (Chatto & Windus, 1997)

Bradshaw's Railway Timetable, 1910 (David & Charles, 1968)

Ship-breakers of Allonby.
Article in Cumberland News, September 1968

C.H. Wylly: The Border Regiment in the Great War (Naval and Military Press, 2003)

Colin Bardgett: The Lonsdale Battalion (1993)

Harvey Broadbent: Gallipoli, the Fatal Shore (Viking, 2005)

Olive Seabury: The Carlisle State Management Scheme (Bookcase, 2007)

Bob Gibson: Silloth Airfield, a Condensed History (Solway Heritage Centre)

Martyn Chorlton: Cumbria Airfields in the Second World War (Countryside Books, 2006)

J.M. Rolfe & K.J. Staples: Flight Simulation (Cambridge Aerospace Series)

Hanley, Boyd and Williamson: An Agricultural Survey of the Northern Province (Armstrong College, Newcastle on Tyne, 1936)

Cumberland Pig Breeders Association Herd Books (Carlisle Library Local Collection)

Geoff Brown: Herdwick Sheep and the Lake District" (Hayloft, 2008)

Jan Levi: And Nobody Woke Up Dead: The Life and Times of Mabel Barker (Ernest Press, 2006)

Mary Scott-Parker: Silloth (Bookcase, 1998)

Stephen White: Solway Steam (Carel Press, Carlisle, 1984)

THE END

Title	ISBN	First published
Chanel and the Tweedmaker Weavers of Dreams	978-0-9572412-2-0	September 2012
Watching over Carlisle 140 years of the Carlisle City Police Force 1827- 1967	978-0-9559017-6-8	July 2011
The Cockermouth Floods a photograpic record	978-09559017-3-7	January 2010
The Keswick and Workington Floods a photographic record	978-09559017-4-4	February 2010
Wetheral and Great Corby an illustrated history	978-09559017-2-0	October 2008
The Carlisle Floods a photographic record	978-09547739-1-5	January 2005
Carlisle Breweries and Public Houses 1894-1916	978-09547739-0-X	2004
Plain People Bygone times on the Solway Plain	978-09548823-1-8	October 2004
More Plain People and places on the Cumbrian Solway Plain	978-09548823-2-7	2007
For more books and further details go to **http://www.p3publications.com** Books can be purchased online using Paypal or credit/debit card		

West beach in the 1950s